Skills FOR

SALES
SUCCESS

Skills FOR SALES SUCCESS

DAVID J. BATCHELOR

ARTHUR H. HORN

IRWIN
PUBLISHING

SKILLS FOR SALES SUCCESS
© CPSA Sales Institute, 1997

Cover and text design:
Matthews Communications Design

Published by
Irwin Publishing
1800 Steeles Avenue West
Concord, Ontario
L4K 2P3

Canadian Cataloguing in Publication Data

Batchelor, David (David J.)
  Skills for sales success

Includes index.
ISBN 0-7725-2280-4
1. Selling   I. Horn, Art.   II. Title
HF5438.25.B37 1996   6585.8'5   C96-931596-1

Printed and bound in Canada

1 2 3 4 5   99 98 97 96

CONTENTS

THE CERTIFIED PROFESSIONAL SALES REPRESENTATIVE (CPSR) PROGRAM

The CPSA Sales Institute was established in 1994 by the Canadian Professional Sales Association in order to promote the vision of professional selling as a respected and recognized career choice. Specifically, the Institute's mission is:

". . . to establish a positive image and enhance the value and credibility of the sales profession by establishing standards, a code of ethics, certification and ongoing professional development programs."

One of the Institute's first achievements was to establish a comprehensive certification process for professional sales representatives across Canada. The result is known as the Certified Professional Sales Representative program, where graduates can earn the professional designation of CPSR. The CPSA Sales Institute acknowledges Human Resources Development Canada (HRDC) for its significant financial contribution to this project and its guidance throughout the development process.

As a CPSR you will:

- be recognized as a designated professional in the field of selling;
- improve your credibility with customers and within your own organization;
- enhance your skill level in the various areas of professional selling;
- increase your productivity and efficiency with job tasks;
- augment your value as an employee;
- improve your self-confidence and self-esteem; and
- strengthen the image of the sales profession as a whole.

To ensure that the certification process effectively prepares individuals to assume careers as sales professionals in Canada, program development was conducted in conjunction with various groups and individuals, including:

- the Canadian Professional Sales Association (CPSA);
- Human Resources Development Canada (HRDC);
- faculty members from various Canadian colleges and universities;
- sales representatives and managers from a cross-section of industries; as well as
- training and consulting professionals specializing in the areas of sales and sales management.

Skills for Sales Success is the result of many months of research and development, and constitutes the primary reference source for the certification process. An Occupational Standards Committee was established by the Institute to oversee the developmental stages of the project, and to set the standards required by sales professionals. Committee members included volunteers from several of the groups listed above. Additional focus groups and validation teams from across Canada were assembled to help establish a comprehensive definition of the core competencies required by sales representatives and sales managers. These competencies were then used by Horn and Associates, a highly recognized training and consulting firm, to define course curriculum and write this textbook.

The Certified Professional Sales Representative program is offered through accredited college and university programs across Canada. The program is also offered directly through the Institute, as a self-study program. Professional sales certification and an official designation are unique to the Canadian marketplace, and serve to distinguish individuals both academically and professionally.

To receive certification and the professional designation of CPSR, candidates must complete a nationwide written and oral examination administered by the CPSA Sales Institute. Completion of the CPSR program at a university or college (or through the self-study program directly through the Institute) is one criterion for participating in the examination process. In order to determine eligibility, applicants are also assessed based on work experience, education and professional development, adherence to the CPSA Sales Institute's professional code of ethics, and various other criteria.

The program is available to seasoned salespeople and managers, individuals new to a vocation in sales, or those considering a professional sales career. A similar program for sales managers is scheduled for launch in the fall of 1997, promoting the designation of Certified Professional Sales Manager (CPSM).

If you are interested in registering for the CPSR program, or need more information about the certification process and eligibility requirements, purchase a copy of this book and call the CPSA Sales Institute at 1-800-268-3794 (in the Toronto area, 416-408-2685).

Dennis Kwasnicki
General Manager

The Challenge

The purpose of this book is to prepare salespeople to write an examination and participate in an oral interview, both of which will test their grasp of the models and interpersonal skills involved in sales success. Those who succeed in these challenges will become certified. Certification will attest to their competence and hard work. It will aid in career development. It will prove that the examinee understands various ethical issues in the field of sales, and commits to comply with certain standards of professional behaviour. It will bring credibility.

But the subject matter is not so easy. Certification requires a keen understanding of several different models and methodologies. It also requires compliance with certain practices and philosophies, all revolving around being genuinely customer-centred while aiming to fulfill performance objectives.

As the information age in which we live advances, the demands on salespeople are growing quickly. Technology, communication, and information volume have combined to challenge and aid salespeople in specific ways.

For one thing, we are now able to define goals and track performance more than ever before. We have to minimize the cost of selling, customer complaints, bad debt, and product returns. We have to maximize volume, margin, contribution, customer retention, return on time invested, referrals, and market share (often in many different ways). The list goes on.

Customers are smarter, it could be argued. They expect more information and expertise from salespeople. They can see through some of the aggressive tactics used by salespeople in the past. They are protected by regulations limiting the games previously endorsed by the hungry

3

selling profession. They have more possible suppliers to choose from, so they can afford to be more demanding.

Some say, "The hard sell is dead."

Modern salespeople are challenged. They have to be experts. They have to do more things than can actually get done. They have to bring value to client relationships. They have to be more scientific, more sophisticated, than ever before as they go about their business.

You may find that some of the processes prescribed in this book are foreign to you. The ideas simply may not fit. For example, some salespeople do not prospect for new customers by calling strangers out of a directory. Instead, they try to penetrate further the companies with which they already do business. Others are simply not in the type of job that requires prospecting or account management at all. Perhaps they handle assigned incoming leads for one-time sales opportunities. Regardless, all salespeople will still benefit from learning the material. Certified means versatile. It could be argued that the best salespeople could sell anything.

In fact, there are many different types of selling vocations. One can sell in a retail environment where staying indoors and dealing with people who walk into the store is the challenge. Others sell for a manufacturer, to corporate end-users. Some represent manufacturers who sell to distributors, who in turn sell to dealers, who ultimately sell to end-users. Some salespeople sell to manufacturers. Some sell over the phone only. Others travel from door to door, on foot. All of these roles require slightly different selling steps.

But the roles all have things in common. They face people who say no, so they have to be able to deal with rejection. They have to balance their own interests with those of their customers. They have to influence people if they want to be successful. They have to be able to communicate well enough to make their customers recognize the value of their products and services. They have to plan how to reach their goals, given a limited amount of time and what are frequently very demanding targets.

This book is written to prepare salespeople to do all of these things and more.

Skills Development

As we'll see in **Part 1: Understanding yourself**, there are a number of personality traits that contribute to sales success. It is important to understand these qualities — and how you can promote them within yourself — before going on to develop the other skills you'll need.

What else does a successful salesperson need? Certainly, in-depth **product and industry knowledge** is important, since this ultimately determines the value of the consulting advice that salespeople are able to offer their customers. But since this type of knowledge is highly specific, it is clearly beyond the scope of this book.

Skills that you need for sales success — and which you will learn here — include the following:

- **Tactical selling skills.** Used when interacting with and, hopefully, influencing customers;
- **Self-management skills.** The ability to manage your time and attitudes;
- **Strategic selling skills.** Used for planning market and account penetration.

Here's a brief preview of what will be covered in these sections.

Part 2: Tactical selling skills

Here we shall consider the basic principles of human influence — the things that "push people's buttons." Then we shall see how these principles are applied to day-to-day selling situations — prospecting for new business, conducting initial sales meetings, presenting finalized ideas, and negotiating transactions.

Part 3: Self-management skills

This section considers everything from how to set goals and manage time to how to manage attitude and stress. Having examined the personality traits of successful salespeople in Part 1, here we'll look at how you can create a more positive outlook, improved performance, and personal success.

Part 4: Strategic selling skills

In perhaps the most demanding section of the book — since strategic skills tend to be less tangible than others — we will focus on selling from both a local and global perspective. In order to be effective in allocating time to various tasks, a salesperson needs to take a "bird's-eye view" of the whole job function or territory (not necessarily geographical). Only with this global thinking process can salespeople address strategic issues, typically expressed by statements such as: *"I need to focus on this particular product, in this particular area, in order to optimize my return on time invested"*; or *"my competitors are hurting me in this area, so I will have to make a plan to compensate."*

The local view prescribed in Part 4 will ask you to consider a plan for one account at a time. Based on things like who is involved in buying decisions, goals for that account, current political situations at the account, and the results of the global analysis, you will be asked to make account plans.

The planning efforts discussed will also be linked to business creation or prospecting activities. Whereas in Part 2: Tactical Selling Skills, prospecting is viewed in terms of contacting prospects and determining a verbal strategy, here prospecting is seen from a big-picture perspective, typified by questions such as: Whom should I call? How do I make sure I'm contacting enough people? Am I staying off the roller coaster of boom and bust caused by uneven prospecting activities? How do I build my list of contacts and how can I manage it?

Administration and reporting are also essential to the strategic side of sales success. Here we will deal with tracking data and performance in order to make better strategic decisions.

EFFORT EQUALS SUCCESS

To sum up, you will find some parts of this book to be challenging, some to be fun, while other parts are quite simple to work through. The material has been designed to prepare participants for the written and oral examinations for CPSR certification. Without reading through this material and doing the work prescribed, it is unlikely you could pass the exam.

Keep in mind that the effort invested in this material could easily yield big returns. In addition to understanding the behaviour employed by some of the world's most successful salespeople, your effort will help you to understand more about yourself. And with CPSR certification, chances are you'll enhance your own career development. You'll be more promotable and more credible. Perhaps the biggest "return" of all will be improved sales productivity.

So have fun.

Take your time.

Do the work.

Keep selling.

Sell even more!

PART 1

UNDERSTANDING YOURSELF

Becoming a successful salesperson is not simply a matter of luck. Evidence suggests that certain personality traits and styles of thinking can significantly affect a person's level of sales success. Research has shown that highly successful salespeople possess similar styles of thinking. And the fact is, everyone shares many of these same qualities. Which ones are your strengths? Which are your weaknesses? That's what we'll be looking at in Part 1.

Understanding your personal qualities is an important first step in achieving sales success. But learning to *manage* and *nurture* these qualities is ultimately your goal — as we'll see more in Part 3: Self-management skills.

Personality Traits for Sales Success

While successful salespeople share a large number of common personality traits, the most important can be described as:

1. Empathy and focus
2. Ego-drive or "hunger"
3. Optimism
4. Attitude toward responsibility

Let's take a look at how these four traits can contribute to sales and
personal success.

➖1 Empathy and focus

More often than not, successful salespeople tend to exhibit high levels
of empathy *and* focus. Note the emphasis on the word "and": these traits
must be balanced, since having too much (or too little) of either trait
can actually be a *hindrance* to sales success.

People who possess a high degree of focus
tend to be *self-oriented* or *inwardly focused* — they
drive consistently towards their own goals. On
the other hand, people who are empathetic will
tend to react with concern for those other than
themselves. Highly empathetic people can be
described as *other-oriented* or *outwardly focused*. It
is important to realize that while individuals

> **By děfǐnǐ'tior**
>
> **Empathy** is the ability to share
> a perspective; to feel what oth-
> ers are feeling.
> **Focus** is, for the purposes of
> this book, a salesperson's goal-
> orientation.

exhibit both of these types of behaviour in various circumstances, most
tend to be oriented predominantly one way or the other.

BALANCE IS CRITICAL

Salespeople benefit from maintaining a *balance* between empathy and
focus. In their consultative role, salespeople need to be empathetic —
directing their attention to the needs of customers. On the other hand,

salespeople can't forget their primary objective — to make the sale and achieve their goals. Developing an appropriate empathy/focus balance makes it easier for salespeople to ensure that both needs are being satisfied.

Let's consider what happens if this balance is not achieved.

Too much empathy. When people are more empathetic than focused, their concern for the needs of others tends to interfere with their ability to drive towards personal goals. In such cases, salespeople stray from their sales objectives, often failing to steer customer conversations adequately. As will be discussed in Part 2, the success of a salesperson has much to do with his or her ability to drive conversations towards establishing customer needs, effectively using this information to make the sale. Consequently, while excessively empathetic salespeople often enjoy good relationships with customers and prospects, they usually suffer from poor sales performance.

Too much focus. Salespeople who are too focused or goal-oriented are generally perceived as being overly aggressive. Focusing attention inward and driving too hard towards closing a sale is likely to make customers feel alienated — they may feel as if their needs and concerns are not being addressed. In these situations, customers may feel pushed or pressured towards making buying decisions. And when customers feel pressured, their egos are more likely to become engaged — they may become defensive and stop listening. So while too much focus and not enough empathy can lead to good initial sales results, it may also result in poor customer relationships and a lack of repeat business.

EMPATHY AND FOCUS IN ACTION

Maintaining balanced, high levels of empathy and focus is not easy. People's personalities tend to dictate whether they are more empathetic or more self-oriented. So, in order to achieve an appropriate balance, you may need to dedicate a significant conscious effort to managing your behaviours and refining your priorities. Once you have achieved an equilibrium, you can work on increasing the levels of both characteristics — you can always become *more* empathetic and *more* focused. The main purpose of balancing empathy and focus is to demonstrate the desire to satisfy customer needs and to establish a clear link between those needs and your product or service. In Part 2, you'll learn about one tool that can assist salespeople in this purpose — an *agenda*. You follow an agenda while linking everything back to the customer/listener.

IMPROVING FOCUS

Poor focus or goal-orientation often results in poor performance and a short-lived sales career. To develop focus, one needs to have goals. Improving focus means improving the ability to get things done. Goals are the "things" to be done. People who lack focus are prone to forget or stray from their purpose. By the same token, driving is pointless without a clear destination. Improving performance requires setting well-defined and achievable goals. Effective goal setting will be examined in Chapter 8.

> ### Quotable...
> *"Don't try to sell what you have . . .*
> *rather have what people need and value."*
> – COMMITMENT TO QUALITY 1992

IMPROVING EMPATHY

Developing a greater level of empathy requires a conscious effort to change one's behaviour. We need to be aware of how self-interest can distract us from focusing our attentions outwardly. Having personal goals is very important, but salespeople must also be able to focus on the needs of their customers. Often, self-interest intrudes on conversations. Indeed, what makes selling difficult is having to set aside one's own self-interests temporarily in favour of someone else's needs.

People with a strong goal-orientation are often reluctant to set aside their personal interests, even temporarily. What they should remember, however, is that setting aside personal interests is *not* the same as losing focus. Selling is all about addressing and serving a customer's needs. And if salespeople are consumed with self-interest, they impede their ability to convey the level of empathy required to provide this customer-oriented service. Ultimately, if a customer does not feel his or her needs are being addressed, the salesperson is less likely to make the sale — and then nobody's interests are served.

LISTENING

Being able to empathize and stay focused involves listening. In fact, one of the most important skills a salesperson can develop is effective listening. Many people hear without actually listening. In order to listen effectively, you must pay attention to what is being communicated and understand what to do with that information. A salesperson must not only listen, but listen with a purpose. Moreover, the ability to understand another person's perspective (needs or interests) requires first knowing what it is.

Writing in the *Harvard Business Review*, psychologist Carl Rogers once suggested that our tendency to evaluate intrudes on our ability to listen and/or communicate. In other words, people tend to be so pre-occupied with wondering what their next move will be, or how they can use what they are hearing, that they actually stop listening to what others are saying. The purpose of listening is to discern relevant information and get to the heart of a matter. For a salesperson, this involves staying on top of the conversation and asking questions — that is, focusing outward. The salesperson should not be thinking *"How will this affect me?"* but rather, *"What is the customer really asking for and how can my product or service satisfy that need?"*

In consultative selling, you must try to link everything back to the customer — ensuring a clear connection between satisfying customer needs and the salesperson's products or services. The key to achieving this link is to balance a strong sense of empathy with a high level of focus.

2 Ego-drive or "hunger"

Another characteristic often shared by successful salespeople is a high level of ego-drive. Ego-drive is essentially measured by your ability to influence others and the strength of your desire to succeed or "win." To evaluate your ego-drive, ask yourself the following questions:

How much hunger do I have to win?
How competitive am I?

MANAGING EGO-DRIVE

A low level of ego-drive is often an indication of unclear goals, a lack of goals altogether, low self-esteem, and/or a lack of motivation. The first step in managing ego-drive is to examine your goals. Goals must be clearly defined and achievable. Goal setting is discussed in detail in Chapter 8.

Once clear goals have been defined or established, it helps to consider what is holding us back from actively striving towards our goals. In other words, we identify the obstacles that cause us *not* to be competitive, or discourage us from driving towards our goals. Once these obstacles are identified, we can implement strategies to remove them.

When low self-esteem is holding back ego-drive, one's attitudes must be examined. In order to nurture a positive attitude and ego-drive, salespeople can practise positive self-talk. Attitude and self-talk will be discussed in more detail in Chapter 7.

◾**3** Optimism

Studies have shown that successful people generally have a high level of optimism — the tendency to look at things from a positive perspective. (Pessimists, on the other hand, are more likely to fail.) As discussed in Martin Seligman's acclaimed book *Learned Optimism*, it is generally accepted within the scientific community that:

> **Quotable...**
> *"It's not the situation . . . it's your reaction to the situation."*
> – BOB CONKLIN
> YOUR ATTITUDE DETERMINES
> YOUR ALTITUDE. 1992

- The way we think, especially about health, changes our health.
- Optimists catch fewer infectious diseases than pessimists.
- Our immune system works better when we are optimistic.
- Optimists tend to live longer than pessimists.

It seems to follow, then, that being optimistic makes sense not only for sales success, but for success at life in general.

CHARACTERISTICS OF OPTIMISM (AND PESSIMISM)

Optimists believe that good fortune is global and pervasive — not a temporary, chance occurrence that only happens to them. In fact, optimists believe that good fortune is shared by everyone. Similarly, an optimist will view misfortune, or bad events, as temporary and localized.

The opposite of an optimist is, of course, a pessimist — someone who habitually believes that misfortune is enduring (permanent), and will undermine everything he or she does (pervasive). Some scientists believe that depression is caused by pessimism and that whether we are pessimistic or not is a matter of habit. Fortunately, we can choose to control our habits.

It is possible to nurture optimism by managing one's self-talk. In order to determine whether your tendency is to be optimistic or pessimistic, ask yourself, *"How do I feel about these things when bad things happen?"* A pessimist's tendency is to generalize — for example, *"No one is buying this product; it's impossible for anyone to sell it."* An optimist is more likely to perceive bad things as being localized, short-term dilemmas to which a *solution* can be found.

Eliminating negative self-talk and ensuring the use of positive self-talk phrases will result in increased optimism. Managing your attitude through self-talk is described in detail in Chapter 7.

▬4▬ Attitude towards responsibility

There are many different types of attitude that affect success. One of the most interesting of these — since it can be easily observed in ourselves and in others — concerns our attitude towards responsibility in the face of problems.

AGENT AND VICTIM BEHAVIOUR

When dealing with problems, people generally fall into one of two categories — victims and agents. When a person's focus is on how a problem is not his or her fault, he or she is exhibiting victim behaviour. People who seek solutions are exhibiting agent behaviour.

For every problem that arises, there is a cause — usually someone's failure to take responsibility or fulfill an intention. Often, those failures can be traced to specific circumstances or to other individuals. However, these reasons are in the past and the problem is in the present. Agents embrace the fact that their role brings with it responsibility. Rather than trying to trace blame, they move forward by creating solutions. Victims focus on proving their lack of blame and responsibility in creating a problem. They are tracing backward, not driving forward or contributing to a solution.

TAKING RESPONSIBILITY

As a salesperson, the foundation of your business is providing solutions, and this requires solution-oriented behaviour. Ask yourself if you are taking or deflecting responsibility. Similar to developing optimism, it is possible to manage and develop agent behaviour by adjusting your self-talk.

A useful illustration can be found at West Point, where it is said that first-year cadets (or "plebes") are allowed to respond to their instructors in only one of three ways: *"Yes, sir!"; "No, sir!"*; and *"No excuses, sir!"* If a cadet fails to complete an assignment, the circumstances are deemed irrelevant; he must always assume responsibility by saying *"No excuses, sir!"* Essentially, the purpose here is to create agent-style thinking.

Individuals can (and should) assume responsibility in a healthy way. It is a matter of choice and self-control. We can become action-oriented, driving towards solutions, recognizing that we have a role and a responsibility in every situation that affects us. Or we can devote our energies to assigning blame or making excuses, which are clearly non-productive efforts.

Admittedly, victims are often realists, providing an accurate perspective in their assessment of what has gone wrong. The problem is that, statistically, they don't do as well in sales, customer service, and management roles. Instead of seeking solutions, victims spend time finding problems, and justifying their innocence. What victims don't understand is that if they are always without blame, they are also always without responsibility. And people tend not to trust, or rely upon, someone without responsibility.

As a rule, customers feel better served when a salesperson exhibits agent behaviour. Agents are perceived as accepting personal responsibility for — and actively working towards — meeting customer needs. Customers need to feel that a salesperson holds himself or herself accountable. They feel frustrated if they are not able to deal with someone who directly controls the situation, and will not perceive themselves to be well served by a salesperson who assumes no responsibility.

OPTIMIST-AGENTS AND PESSIMIST-VICTIMS

Optimists typically display agent behaviour. They view problems as local, and are willing to acknowledge responsibility without loss of self-esteem. As agents, optimists see that they can seek solutions to problems, which they view as temporary; for example: *"People are spending less, so I will have to find special value in my product for my customers to maintain my level of sales."* Pessimists habitually believe that misfortune is enduring and undermines all they do. In this way, they are deflecting personal responsibility for problems by blaming them on general or universal misfortune; for example: *"Nobody is buying anything anymore. I can't possibly maintain my sales levels."* They are displaying victim behaviour.

FOLLOWING THROUGH

An important part of being agents involves doing what we have resolved to do. Following through on our intentions is an integral part of being responsible. Essentially, doing what we intend to do is a "thinking style" and, like agent and victim behaviour, it can be developed and nurtured.

Doing what you intend to do is a matter of keeping your word, to yourself and to others. If you say you will do something, and you retain the conviction to do it, you will build credibility and respect. That's not as easy as it sounds, since it sometimes means doing things you'd rather not do. It also requires maintaining your focus in situations that can be distracting or conflicting.

There are practical ways to ensure that we do the things we intend to do. We can create a *closed-loop system* for managing our activities. This involves making notes about the things we have agreed to do for others, or the promises and goals we have made to ourselves. Notes act as reminders and guides for acting on our intentions. A closed-loop system allows you to define tasks and steps towards fulfilling your word, or intentions. It allows you to refer to your promises, as a reminder, and to ensure that they are kept. Details about closed-loop systems will be examined in our discussion of time management in Chapter 9.

SUMMARY

1. This introductory chapter describes several of the key personality traits that are common to successful salespeople. Developed properly, these can help to achieve high performance.

2. Take the time to look inwardly. Evaluate your personality in light of each of the areas discussed, then decide which traits need to be changed and which can be used to your advantage. Develop a list of things you plan to do over the next year regarding your personality. As you accomplish each objective (or feel you have), cross it off the list and start on the next one. Keep in mind that changing certain aspects of your personality takes time, and you shouldn't try to address too much at once. Therefore, set priorities in your list and take things one at a time.

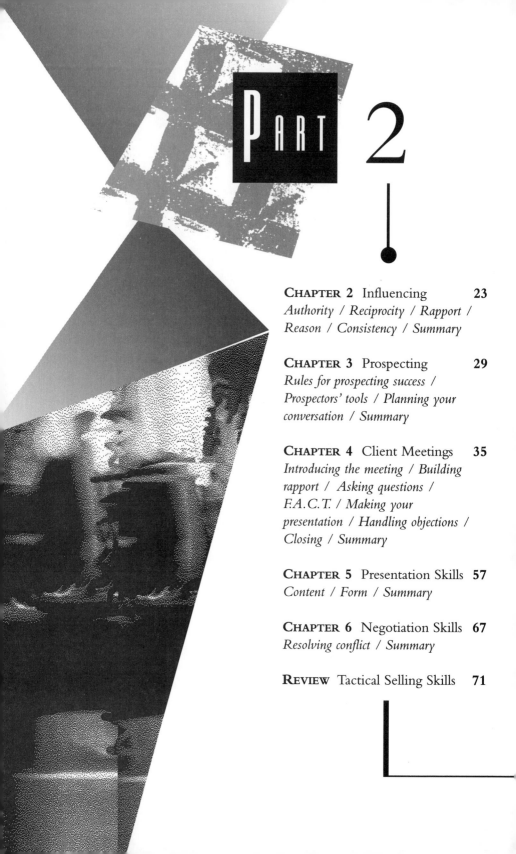

PART 2

TACTICAL SELLING SKILLS

Tactical skills are used when salespeople interact with clients or customers — in face-to-face situations, over the telephone, or even over the Internet. These skills are the first of the three primary skill sets required of successful salespeople. The other two — self-management and strategic skills — coupled with product knowledge, make up the remaining requirements for sales success.

In this section, we will examine tactical selling skills in order, matching the traditional sequence of steps in the selling process. Typically, salespeople will create new customer relationships by making the first contact, building rapport, asking questions, benefit selling, handling objections, closing, and following up on the sale. The final chapters in this section will address tactical skills in this sequence.

Influencing

In this chapter we will consider the theoretical foundation of the tactical skills covered in this section. We'll look at the various ways in which humans influence each other, and therefore how salespeople influence customers.

Social psychologists have undertaken considerable research into what "causes compliance" — creating what is generally referred to as *compliance theory*. This model describes why each of the tactical selling skills covered here actually works. Compliance theory is at the heart of selling. If salespeople master basic tools for causing compliance, they will be able to sell more.

Compliance tactics exist because they contribute to the survival and evolution of the species. Humans are born with certain traits programmed into their thinking. Other traits are more likely to be taught by caregivers and subsequently reinforced by society.

In this course of study, we shall consider five primary tools for causing compliance (or "influencing people"). We shall list these tools, one at a time, and explain their applications.

1 Authority

The principle of authority states that people will generally follow the advice of someone who is recognized as having expertise, or who holds an important position within a hierarchy. Babies tend to respond favourably to (or *comply* with) loud, deep voices. This response has helped infants to survive. In the same way, perhaps as a result of the same programming, adults tend to comply with the suggestions of experts such as doctors or lawyers or other professionals who are perceived as knowledgeable. Perceived authority elicits respect and, ultimately, compliance. We follow the advice of people we respect.

The Ethics of Compliance

In considering the tools that cause customer compliance, various ethical issues arise concerning their use. An unethical salesperson, for example, might make a false statement just to effect a sale, even though it is counter to the best interests of the customer and the community.

This text assumes that salespeople will adhere to one of the basic rules of social and business protocol: *be honest*. (Note that we are already using a compliance tactic here; it is called *social evidence*, meaning that we tend to do what we believe other people tend to do.) If, for example, it is clear to you that by telling customers your product is in short supply (another compliance tactic: *scarcity*) you will increase their interest in that product, then you are able to cause compliance simply by making the claim. Clearly, however, such a tactic should be used only if the claim is in fact true.

Ultimately, the ethics of selling are left up to salespeople themselves, who are frequently faced with ethical dilemmas regarding what they say. Resolving these dilemmas is simply a matter of ensuring that you tell the truth.

For example, research shows that people who want to cross from one side of a street to the other are more likely to follow a jaywalker if he or she is dressed in a nurse's uniform or a postal uniform, than if the jaywalker is dressed casually. Somehow, we perceive that the uniform projects authority.

Similarly, when your customers perceive that you "know your stuff," they will have more confidence in you. Some salespeople are more effective than others at conveying this sense of authority.

How effective are you at projecting competence or authority? Here are some things to consider:

- Does your business card show a title that projects expertise, seniority, or authority?
- Do you pay attention to your appearance?
- Do you know your products well?
- Do you help your customers solve problems and reach goals?
- If you have a lot of experience in your industry, do you mention it to your prospective customers?

2 Reciprocity

Reciprocity is the compliance tactic that elicits a sense of indebtedness for having received a favour. It derives from our sense of fairness, reflected by statements such as "you scratch my back, I'll scratch yours." This is a human tendency that is nurtured by parents and by society and contributes to the survival of the species.

Reciprocity goes to the very core of the capitalistic spirit. We adhere to the notion that "fair is fair": that charging a fair price for value is the way to do business, and that by bringing added value to customers, salespeople will keep their business — that is, their customers' compliance.

It is incumbent upon salespeople, therefore, to serve their established customers well and to act in their ultimate, long-term best interests in order to create and sustain this bond. By also going out of your way to bring value to new potential relationships, you create bonds that can ultimately lead to new business.

3 Rapport

The principle of building rapport is based on the fact that we generally follow the advice of people we like. This derives from another ingrained human tendency: to assemble into clans or groups with shared values or missions. In other words, we are drawn to people who are like ourselves.

Commonality is the feeling that there are things in common between people. There are four accepted levels of commonality which salespeople can attempt to achieve.

The first level concerns *shared interest*, generally arrived at by what is known as "small talk." For example, at the outset of meetings with clients and prospects, salespeople will often spend time building rapport by discussing everything from the weather to last summer's fishing trip. They do this to build a bond.

The second way in which salespeople can build commonality is through their *style of speech*. If a customer perceives, consciously or unconsciously, that the salesperson speaks the same way or uses the same jargon as he or she does, a bond is likely to be built between the two parties.

The third way to establish unconscious or conscious feelings of commonality is by *mirroring posture*. The idea here is that people who stand, sit, or hold their bodies in similar ways will feel a kind of bond with each other.

The fourth (and most subtle) way to build rapport with customers is to share their *style of thinking*. If two people feel that they share similar perspectives, then they are likely to build a common bond.

◀4▶ Reason

As a compliance tactic, "reason" is based on our natural tendency to respond to requests that make sense. Why humans tend to comply with sensible arguments is virtually self-explanatory: we are motivated by survival; and if a particular act helps us to survive, we will generally perform that act.

The challenge for salespeople in employing the compliance tactic of reason is to ensure that their logical arguments — or benefit selling — are clear to the customer. One way to do this is to remind a customer of his or her goal, and then show why your proposal is the most efficient means of attaining that goal.

> **By dĕfĭnĭ'tĭon**
>
> **Efficiency.** Gaining high outputs in return for relatively lower inputs; that is, big returns on minimal expenditure.

Notice that the concept of *efficiency* goes hand in hand with the concept of reason. To use a simple example, let's say that you want a chocolate bar. It is rational for you to go to the nearest store to buy one. Going to a store on the other side of town, however, would not be rational because it is not efficient.

Demonstrating to customers the efficiency of your product or service allows you to use the compliance tactic of reason to gain agreement.

◀5▶ Consistency

As a rule, people behave consistently with their self-concepts, with their previous behaviour, and with commitments they have made. Salespeople should therefore remind customers that their product or service is congruent with the way customers see themselves, how it is consistent with previous steps taken, and how it fulfills previously cited intentions and promises.

Animals in nature tend to behave in ways that they have behaved in the past, as long as that behaviour was not harmful. A moose in the forest takes the same path to the water's edge when it seeks a drink; this practice has been successful for the animal so far, so its continuation is sensible. For the same reason, humans tend to behave consistently. Life is somewhat easier when we do as we did before, or when we do as we intended or promised.

Of course, this is not to say that customers won't decide to break away from established patterns. Indeed, a customer's decision may be just for the sake of change or because of various other compliance phenomena. Sometimes it is simply the strongest impulse that wins.

On the other hand, the impulse to fulfill a commitment can be particularly strong. In fact, the clearer the commitment, the stronger the propensity to fulfill it. Salespeople use this compliance tactic to their advantage when they ask customers questions intended to close a sale. They deliberately elicit a commitment to proceed so that, ultimately, the customer is less likely to change his or her mind. As we will see later, a "wishy-washy" suggestion of intention provides little motivation to act.

Salespeople use consistency as a compliance tactic when they find a way to remind customers of the means by which they can behave consistently, or extract a self-concept or commitment. Also, when salespeople behave consistently with their commitments, they encourage (through the tactic of reciprocity) their customers to act in kind.

SUMMARY

1. Compliance theory is at the centre of selling. Whenever someone influences someone else, a compliance tactic is at work.

2. We have looked closely at five compliance tactics:

   - authority;
   - reciprocity;
   - rapport;
   - reason; and
   - consistency.

We made passing reference to two others:

   - scarcity; and
   - social evidence.

3. All of these tactics, and others not mentioned, involve the various skills involved in tactical selling. They are simply a different way of organizing these skills. Traditional sales manuals list selling skills as a series of steps to take. Here, as compliance tactics, they are arranged based on the overall effect they cause.

4. Compliance tactics work; they have led to the success of the species. *Authority* has kept us alive because it has caused us to listen to those worthy of respect. *Reciprocity* has created the bonds that make civilization work. *Rapport* leads to attraction between different individuals and to the creation of social units. *Reason* directs people to do what helps them survive and reach goals. *Consistency* has kept us safe from the risk of the unpredictable.

5. When salespeople employ compliance tactics, they attempt to play off natural human tendencies. This raises the moral question of whether it is fair to say something to someone, knowing that what you say will cause them to act in a predictable fashion. The answer is to use compliance tactics *honestly*, helping people to reach their goals. This is how consultative selling works.

Prospecting

Prospecting is the process by which a salesperson gets new customers. Also known as cold calling, hunting steel, or pounding the pavement, prospecting can be one of the most challenging components of a salesperson's job.

In this chapter we will be studying the interpersonal elements of prospecting. (Later, in Part 4, we'll look at how to manage prospecting activities, how to ensure an optimum return on prospecting time invested, and how to generate lists of prospecting targets.)

For simplicity's sake, we'll assume that you do your prospecting over the telephone. Of course, some salespeople make their first approach to customers face-to-face; in such cases, however, they require all the skills needed in successful telephone prospecting, as well as the ability to handle initial face-to-face meetings. (We'll look at the topic of first meetings in Chapter 4.)

RULES FOR PROSPECTING SUCCESS

Before dealing with the actual process of planning and making your initial customer contact, let's consider a few basic rules for successful prospecting. **Make the time.** While different sales positions vary in their requirements, prospecting is usually expected to account for about 20 percent of the salesperson's time. This allocation (equal to one day a week) is difficult for many salespeople. One reason may be private fear of rejection; another may be simple forgetfulness. Sometimes we just become so consumed by day-to-day urgent demands that the important tasks are left undone. (Effective time management is discussed in Part 3.) Ultimately, prospecting success depends on the *principle of activity* — if you don't contact new prospects on a regular basis, then you obviously won't generate many new customers. The bottom line here is simple: "keep moving." If you want to enjoy long-term sales success, then you have to make a regular effort to contact new customers — no matter how painful the effort is.

Take it step by step. Don't expect to make the sale on your first call. In fact, it is generally unwise to solicit an actual sale over the telephone. The initial goal of many prospecting calls is simply to get the customer's permission to send him or her a piece of correspondence, some company information, or to call back at a more convenient time. Successful prospectors establish a specific, short-term goal, then aim to achieve it — and only it. Taking this step-by-step approach makes prospecting a less daunting task. It is much easier to ask someone for permission to stay in touch than it is to request a meeting (let alone a commitment to buy). Getting that permission still requires the necessary skills — getting to the point quickly, for example, or demonstrating potential value to the customer — but you'll be much less likely to procrastinate if you stick with manageable goals.

Be enthusiastic.   A flat, uninteresting message delivered in a soft, monotone voice is unlikely to generate much prospecting success. As a rule, keep your prospecting calls upbeat, attractive to the prospect (offering value — things the prospect is interested in), and focused on fulfilling the mission of the call. They must be geared towards building commonality at the outset.

Listen carefully. Another key to prospecting success lies in listening skills. Salespeople need to listen extremely well while driving towards their own goals, striking a balance between empathy and focus. (These concepts are described in Chapter 1.) If you appear more concerned about attaining you own goals than about what the prospect has to say, you will come across as pushy and unattractive. Focus instead on the prospect's interests and situation at the time of the call, so that you can address his or her needs. Such empathy goes a long way towards establishing rapport, a sense of reciprocity, and ultimately, the potential for a long-term customer relationship.

Be able to deal with rejection. Prospecting means soliciting business from people who are essentially strangers. So it's not surprising that salespeople frequently face rejection. And because rejection is a uniquely painful experience, the ability to deal with rejection — to remain persistent and focused — is critical to prospecting success. (In Part 3, we'll examine the self-management skills required to handle the rejection that prospectors regularly face.)

Prospecting relies upon many of a salesperson's tactical and strategic selling skills. In addition to those situations already discussed, for example, you may need to address a customer's objections or drive the conversation towards a logical (beneficial) conclusion or close. You might have to discuss the features and corresponding benefits of the products and services in question. And so on.

Prospecting success is linked to many of the skills that will be examined later in this book. In fact, once you have finished reading this book, you may want to review this chapter in order to synthesize the information from the chapters that follow. In this way, you may enhance your prospecting or cold-calling activities even further.

PROSPECTORS' TOOLS

Successful prospecting requires more than just picking up the phone (although this step is ultimately necessary!). Some salespeople will send prospects a personal letter before contacting them. If appropriate, they may enclose a gift or brochure with the letter to create a top-of-mind impression that will be recalled when they initiate contact. The most important thing is that whatever goes out to prospects be perfect in all respects. That means concise, diplomatic writing; perfect grammar; proper letter layout; and appropriate envelope presentation. No less vital are clean photocopies, properly stapled or paper-clipped — even the placement of the stamp on the envelope is critical!

In advance of the actual phone call, it is important to assemble the basic requirements of the call. Reference materials, customer files, writing instruments, calculators, price schedules, and brochures are all-important tools, depending on the industry and nature of the call. Any additional tools used to record the results of the call are also valuable.

Some salespeople employ a computerized activity-monitoring tool which allows them to record the results of their calls and set up reminders to make future contacts or conduct further activities concerning each prospect. The habit of setting down the next steps to take, whether in a computerized or manual format, is critical.

It is also important to make notes about what you have learned during prospect calls. This helps to remind you of what was discussed when you make your next call, thereby creating an air of professionalism and saving time for both you and your prospect.

PLANNING YOUR CONVERSATION

The success of a cold call is determined in the first few seconds of contact. So it is important to plan your conversation ahead of time. Some key questions to consider as you plot your approach are:

- What do I know about the prospect that I can use to start the conversation?
- What does this prospect have in common with my other clients?
- What do I know about this contact?
- Why am I calling?
- Can my organization help the prospect, and in what way?
- Are there other contacts to mention?
- What sort of needs might the prospect possess?
- What are my call objectives? (for example, permission to contact someone else, setting an appointment, uncovering current or future needs)
- What questions will I ask?
- What objections might the prospect raise, and what will my responses be?

Although it is not necessary to script your prospecting calls (a script can sound contrived and may undermine the salesperson's ability to answer the customer's questions), it *is* valuable to set out (in point form) comments or ideas that need to be covered. Use the list of questions shown above to help you prepare.

Early in your call, be sure to provide the prospect with a link to who you are — things you have in common, mutual contacts, reference sources. It is also important to state, up front, the value of what you have to offer. Saying that you provide products similar to what the customer is purchasing now probably won't do much to sustain your conversation. Instead, you must differentiate your organization from the competition in order to justify the prospect's time. On the other hand, as you'll see on page 33 (The 5 Don'ts of Cold Calling), any claims you do make must be done tactfully, or you risk provoking a dispute.

The 5 Don'ts of Cold Calling

1. Don't launch into a monologue.

It takes a few seconds for a prospect's hearing and thinking to catch up with your speech. Therefore, even though the first moments of a call are the most valuable — that is the point where the prospect forms an opinion of you and what you have to offer — be sure to start your conversation with broad statements. Focus on making a favourable impression and gaining the prospect's interest in hearing more before you launch into the body of your presentation. Give the prospect time to catch up with you, and then start a two-way conversation.

2. Don't make outrageous claims.

Making excessively bold claims can give the prospect points to argue and put you on the defensive. Being confident is one thing, but arrogant statements will probably alienate the prospect. Instead of saying "I know I can," for example, try saying something like "I am very confident that we can . . ."

3. Don't sound canned.

In a cold call, you want to appear genuine, helpful, and direct. Consequently, you shouldn't use canned conversation; it sounds insincere and doesn't carry much meaning. One method of avoiding such conversation is to vary your sales pitch frequently. It is also valuable to rehearse the opening of your prospecting call to the point where it sounds as natural as possible. Some salespeople use a tape recorder to review their tone of voice. They practise this until they can hear themselves sounding natural, yet controlled and focused.

4. Don't burn bridges.

Sometimes salespeople are overly abrupt or curt with personnel who answer the phone on behalf of the targeted prospect. Ultimately, these front-line individuals can be critical allies in your efforts to win business; it is wise to treat them accordingly.

5. Don't use jargon.

Prospective customers are turned off by representatives who use excessive jargon and/or excessively technical language. Often, a salesperson's organization or industry has its own terminology — one that might not be universally applicable. Be sure to speak at the customer's level of understanding. Jargon may be acceptable only if the customer is familiar and comfortable with it.

Finally, make sure your contact knows that you will be discreet with any information that he or she shares with you. If you talk too much about what you have done for other organizations, the prospect might logically conclude that someday his or her company will be the subject of conversation with another potential customer.

SUMMARY

1. Procrastination — because of fear of rejection or other factors — is a common obstacle to successful prospecting.

2. Prospecting becomes a less daunting task, however, when seen as an opportunity to present potential customers with solutions to their problems and tools to achieve their goals. Salespeople need not see prospecting as an attempt to make an immediate sale; it should be viewed as an attempt to start a relationship based on a mutual recognition of value to be exchanged.

3. The key to successful cold calling is to make clear at the outset how you and your products are different from — and better than — what the customer is using now (without knocking the competition). Somehow find a way to justify the phone conversation. Start with some link (commonality), and when the customer appears more focused on what is going on, ease into what makes you special.

4. Prospecting is about building relationships; the first phone call is usually to get a commitment to a next step — perhaps a first appointment, a subsequent phone call, a call to another player in the prospect's company, or even just permission to send a letter or brochure. You need not ask for the world — just permission to take another step based on the clear possibility of adding value to a customer's situation.

Client Meetings

When meeting with a prospect or when meeting with clients on an ongoing basis, most salespeople follow a natural sequence of steps:

- **Introduce the meeting.** Make statements about the purpose of the meeting and provide a context for the conversation.
- **Build rapport.** Early in the conversation, spend time to establish or reinforce the customer relationship.
- **Ask questions.** Eventually, the meeting proceeds to a point where the salesperson can ask questions to uncover client needs. The purpose here is to determine whether there is a match between what the client requires and what the salesperson has to offer.
- **Make the sales presentation.** Here the salesperson proceeds to sell his or her products or ideas. Doing so involves describing the benefits that the products offer the customer — that is, the value the customer will receive by making the desired purchase.
- **Handle objections.** Often, customers respond to a sales presentation by raising various concerns, or objections. It is the salesperson's task to address these concerns.
- **Close.** After dealing with any customer concerns, the salesperson attempts to gain the customer's commitment to some next step.

This series of steps has remained essentially unchanged since the early 1900s. Why? Because it reflects how humans tend to interact. We establish our reason for talking, while building a sense of rapport. We uncover the mission of the other party. We discuss that mission in terms of how we might contribute. We deal with various concerns and we make commitments towards some next step. This is how humans help one another reach goals.

In this chapter, we'll be examining each of these steps in the order described above. Of course, the sequence may vary in real-life situations

Consultative Selling

Throughout the history of selling, the sales profession has moved cyclically from a hard-sell (or salesperson-dominant) approach to one that is softer, more consultative (or customer-centred). Since the 1980s a basic consultative method has been employed. This has meant essentially that the customer is more important than the sale (versus the hard-sell style, in which the sale is more important than the customer). One of the basic principles of consultative selling is that the customer is the "star of the show."

In this consultative context — that is, where the salesperson is acting as a consultant trying to fulfill the customer's best interests — salespeople rely less on their own agendas and more on the customer's objectives. However, when customer-created digressions have been addressed, a salesperson with strong focus will be able to return to the agenda described on the previous page.

— a versatile salesperson will often jump from one step to another, depending on his or her perception of what is appropriate in the circumstances. For example, a customer might raise objections while the salesperson is establishing context for the meeting. Although this step is out of order from the standard agenda, successful salespeople address these initial objections and then go back to build rapport and restate the purpose of the meeting.

Similarly, if a salesperson is asking questions to uncover customer needs, the customer may also have questions — say, concerning the benefits of the salesperson's product. Even though the salesperson has not finished asking questions, he or she should ensure that the customer's questions have been answered and concerns addressed.

Clearly, the order of the steps is less important than the steps themselves. So let's take a look at each one in detail.

INTRODUCING THE MEETING

Not long after starting his or her conversation with the customer, the salesperson makes introductory comments to establish the context of the meeting (how it came about, its general mission, etc.), and the steps he or she plans to follow (for example, "I'd like to ask you several questions to help me understand your needs; then perhaps I can suggest how I might be able to assist you, so that we can determine if we can work together..."). Next, the salesperson verifies the time available to the customer, and then states his or her specific goal.

Customers generally appreciate having the context of the meeting established, and they feel drawn to salespeople who give them a clear view of how their time is about to be spent.

BUILDING RAPPORT

Much of a salesperson's success depends on his or her ability to establish a warm relationship with a customer. If there is not a sense of trust between two parties, those parties are not likely to do business together. Therefore, at the beginning of most customer interactions — in fact, throughout the entire relationship — a salesperson will take steps to reinforce this human bond.

It is important for salespeople to build relationships authentically — as you'll recall from Chapter 1, salespeople have a responsibility to deal honestly with their customers. Salespeople often wrestle with the question of whether they can be honest and build relationships with people whom they do not particularly like. For example, they might ask, *"Can I pretend to be friendly when I feel unfriendly towards a person?"*

But friendliness really isn't the issue. You needn't pretend to be friendly. The challenge is to express a genuine concern for the other person. You may not foresee a natural friendship evolving, but you can still sincerely try to help the other person, tell the truth, and maintain integrity in the relationship. The trick is to ignore whatever dislike you may feel and switch on your natural capacity for empathy. Building rapport in this manner is not a manipulative technique to make people like you; it is a skill designed to ensure that your interest in building genuine relationships can be fulfilled.

Keep in mind, too, that there are benefits to establishing a rapport with people other than your customers. It should extend to colleagues and internal support personnel. Indeed, you'll find that gaining the support of internal departments such as expediting, credit, manufacturing, shipping, marketing — even company management — is almost as important as building healthy relationships with existing and prospective customers.

There are four essential elements to building rapport:
- projecting honesty;
- demonstrating competence;
- showing propriety; and
- building commonality.

Let's examine each element in detail.

◢**1** Honesty

If we want to build a trusting relationship with our customers, it is critical that they recognize our honest intentions. But how? It is one thing to be honest in conversation; making sure the customer perceives this honesty is another thing altogether.

Of course, we can just hope that the customer recognizes honesty. But there are things you can to do help that recognition.

For example, you might go out of your way to point out ways that the customer can benefit from a certain idea — even if it's not in your best interests. Let's say that the customer is interested in one of your products, but you believe that the product is really not appropriate to the customer's needs. Admitting this to your customer will go a long way toward demonstrating your honesty.

◢**2** Competence

Salespeople project competence by establishing themselves as experts or authorities in a given area. (Recall the compliance tactic of authority, which we discussed in Chapter 2.) You can do this by asking intelligent questions and by recounting your experience (as humbly as possible). An example of this approach might be, *"I've been looking at these kinds of situations for over twelve years and I've never seen a solution to that particular problem; the best I've ever heard of is —."*

Citing the expertise of other personnel inside the salesperson's company is another way to project competence — for example, *"We have a team of technical experts backing us up who provide this kind of service to our customers."*

The key to projecting competence, however, is to have it — through excellent product knowledge, and the ability to bring value to client interactions. Ideally, after each contact with you, your customers should be thinking to themselves: "Gosh, I got something valuable from that conversation." Once again, in the consultative model, sales is not a matter of flogging products. It is a matter of bringing value to customers in excess of what they actually pay for your products or services. As a result, everyone benefits — the customer, the salesperson, the salesperson's employer, and the economy as a whole.

▬3 Propriety

A salesperson who demonstrates propriety is someone who behaves appropriately, or according to certain accepted social norms. This can include what you wear (the general rule is to match or slightly exceed the customer's level of dress), and following basic rules of social etiquette. Failure to adhere to standards of propriety will almost certainly affect your ability to establish rapport with a customer.

▬4 Commonality

As discussed in Chapter 2, salespeople establish a rapport with customers by: sharing interests; adopting certain physical stances; adopting similar styles of speech; and, most importantly, thinking in ways that are similar to the customer's. This latter skill is not so much pretending a point of view; rather, it is simply the adoption of a style that will be readily appreciated by the customer. One might visualize the customer's mind as having entry points of varying shapes and sizes. It is the salesperson's job to "shape" his or her ideas in a manner that will fit those entry points. The ideas just won't make it in if they are not properly shaped.

Ultimately, it is more important to speak the customer's language than your own. (Remember that empathy is a primary personality trait of successful salespeople.) If you cannot speak the customer's language, if you cannot make the customer feel understood, or if you cannot tailor your style to match the needs and expectations of the

✔ *Personal Check*

DOs and DON'Ts of propriety

☐ DO shake hands firmly.

☐ DO keep eye contact.

☐ DO be on time.

☐ DO be neatly attired.

☐ DO ensure that you are well-groomed.

☐ DO make notes of commitments.

☐ DO keep your promises.

☐ DON'T use humour based on race, colour, creed, or sex.

☐ DON'T start conversations about sex, politics, or religion.

☐ DON'T ask for coffee or refreshments without being offered.

☐ DON'T ask for permission to smoke.

☐ DON'T refer to women as "girls."

☐ DON'T use profanity of any sort.

customer, you will fail to establish a sense of trust. Making customers feel understood is a primary requirement for sales success.

But how do we actually go about matching the customer's style of thinking? Well, one simple method is to repeat to customers in your own words what you hear them saying. This allows customers to feel understood, and it allows you to confirm your own understanding of what is being said.

Another means of establishing commonality at this level is to take the customer's ideas and concerns further than already stated by the customer. This enhances your perceived competence, as well as the customer's recognition that you are in tune with his or her needs and objectives.

Yet another means by which salespeople can establish commonality is to speak in ways that will appeal to the customer. For example, if a customer appears to have a substantial ego, it makes sense to respond to his or her need to feel important. Where a customer tends to procrastinate, helping him or her to put things into motion will probably facilitate the sale. Some customers like to analyze and pursue details, so you should provide these in appropriate quantity. If customers are soft-spoken, you should deliver your messages in a comparable tone.

For many years, psychologists have attempted to categorize people according to their personal characteristics or styles of behaviour. One such characteristic is the speed of a person's movements, speech, or thinking. (Someone who thinks or speaks quickly likes to be approached at a relatively fast pace; a person who speaks or thinks slowly requires a comparably leisurely approach.) People can also be categorized according to whether they take a logical or emotional approach to matters.

These two characteristics—speed and logical/emotional orientation — can be graphed to create a matrix of four personality types, as shown in Figure 4.1 (opposite page).

The **DRIVER** is a relatively fast moving, logical thinker. Drivers need to be approached with the same style they possess themselves, although this cannot be competitive or confrontational, just logical and fast.

The **ANALYTICAL** type requires a somewhat more studied approach to matters, where issues are broken down into their logical components and methodically addressed.

An **AMIABLE** personality type is someone who moves somewhat more slowly; amiable types are more feeling-oriented, and require an appeal to their softer sides.

Figure 4.1

The Theory of Social Styles
A graphic matrix of two personality dimensions: speed of thinking and logical reasoning.

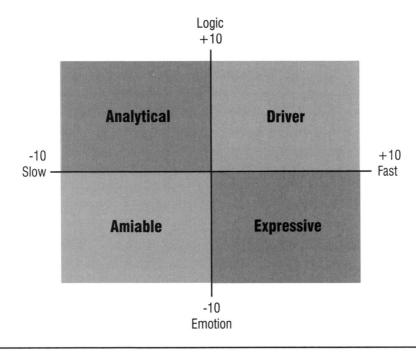

Adapted from "The Theory of Social Styles." SOURCE: *Personal Styles And Effective Performance: Making Your Style Work For You*, David Merrill & Roger Reid, © 1981.

The EXPRESSIVE type may require a somewhat faster, louder (or more emotional), and communicative relationship.

These categories can be helpful for identifying various customer styles and modifying your own style accordingly. For example, in order to appeal to a driver-type customer, an amiable-type salesperson must overcome his or her natural inclination to a relaxed, feelings-oriented approach. He or she will need to work at being more logical and to the point.

Personal-style categories are helpful in enabling salespeople to assess customers rapidly, adapt to a customer's style, and thereby build rapport. Keep in mind, however, that the categorization process is necessarily oversimplified — after all, human personalities consist of a lot more than two variables. Moreover, it is arguably unfair to label people. So it makes sense to view this model (which we'll call a simplified version of the *Theory of Social Styles*) as just a useful tool for making rapid, tentative, "unofficial" assessments of how you can build customer rapport.

Asking questions

Once you've established the context of the client meeting and spent some time building customer rapport, the next step is to ask questions that will uncover the information you need to develop a successful sale.

Here it's worth remembering that business is driven by progress, which means businesspeople are usually trying to get somewhere. They're trying to solve a problem, trying to become bigger, more profitable, or generally more successful. Very rarely are businesspeople happy where they are. So your challenge as a salesperson is to uncover exactly why customers are not where they want to be, and to illustrate the link between their needs and your products or services.

If you can define what your customer needs, it puts you in a clear position to decide whether you can help. Or, if you clearly understand the customer's goal, you can determine how to help fulfill that goal.

Clearly, in order to take full advantage of the questioning opportunity, you need to know exactly what will be required to secure the customer's business. Successful salespeople focus on how customers like to make decisions and on how they like to process information. Sometimes it can be advantageous to ask outright: *"What will it take for us to work together here?"*

Areas of questioning that typically yield useful information are shown in the Personal Check box at left. All of these questions usually need to be answered by the end of a first meeting with a customer.

It is important to ask your questions tactfully. For example, you cannot say to a buyer, *"So, who makes the final decision?"* Such a question might be offensive to someone who would like to think of himself or herself as having that authority. Perhaps a better way to ask

---

☑ *Personal Check*

Asking the right questions

☐ Exactly what does the customer need?

☐ Are there budgetary issues?

☐ Who's involved in making the decision and what will their individual goals and concerns be?

☐ What is the timing of the possible purchase?

☐ What are the steps involved in getting the sale?

☐ What are the criteria for making the decision on suppliers?

this particular question would be, *"Aside from my need to gain your support for this relationship, who else needs to be onside?"*

Support statements are comments you make throughout the questioning process that keep the level of tact high and the conversation progressing comfortably for the customer. For example, if a customer says that things around his or her organization have been really hectic lately, it would be prudent to comment on the observation. It sends the signal that you care and that you are listening.

Support statements, when used as clauses that preface a question, can also serve to justify or demonstrate the rationale for a line of questioning. For example, to ask a potentially awkward question like, *"How have sales been for you lately?"* you might start the question with a comment: *"You mentioned how hectic it has been around here lately; is that a sign that sales have been going well?"*

Asking questions effectively poses yet another challenge to the salesperson's ability to empathize with the customer while remaining focused. Support statements are empathetic gestures that preface the salesperson's efforts to focus on what needs to be uncovered to secure the sale. Authentic empathy for the customer's situation yields the information required to focus on providing solutions.

As always, however, you need to keep empathy and focus in balance. If empathy is too high, questioning just triggers digression. If focus is too high, questioning seems like interrogation. Nevertheless, questioning is a significant opportunity to sharpen your focusing skills. As long as it is accompanied by keen listening and compassion, it can go a long way towards establishing credibility and uncovering exactly what it takes to be successful in your mission.

Salespeople with high levels of focus generally anticipate the sale before walking into a client meeting. This is not to say that you should decide what will be sold before the customer's needs are uncovered (remember, the idea is to be consultative). But you should have sufficient focus to know what you want to sell.

Once you've determined the product or service to be sold, you need to find out how it will solve the customer's problem, or help the customer to reach his or her goal. For example, if your mission is to sell a broom, you know that the broom's function is to sweep dirty floors. Here, you simply approach the customer, raise the topic of dusty floors, and proceed to sell your broom.

You must be prepared, however, to discover a client need that may be different from what you had anticipated. This is the essence of an empathetic or consultative approach; pressing on with your agenda regardless of customer need is overly focused — in short, too "hard sell."

If you're selling services instead of products, you are sometimes not in a position to walk into a client meeting with a particular solution in mind. In this situation, you need to uncover exactly what problems customers need to have solved or what goals need to be fulfilled. A good salesperson will then rapidly assimilate customer situations and produce tentative ideas (on the spot) that bring value to the client conversation. In this sense, the salesperson is a true consultant, delivering fresh ideas oriented toward solving problems and fulfilling goals for other people.

Notice, however, that in both the preceding scenarios — that is, where you know what you want to sell before you walk in, and where you uncover goals and create solutions on the spot — it is necessary to focus on *your* goal and use a series of steps to attain that goal. Both require an agenda, and use the same line of questioning.

F.A.C.T.

One method by which salespeople follow a line of reasoning when questioning a customer is known by the acronym, F.A.C.T. It is based on the idea that, by asking a series of general questions — which, metaphorically speaking, seem to circle in the air looking for the appropriate problem — salespeople can determine the customer's greatest concern or most important goal. Hence, the salesperson attempts to

Find the problem, then proceeds to ...

Analyze the nature of that problem; then, in order to raise the customer's motivation to address that problem, asks him or her to ...

Consider the consequences of the problem; thereafter, with the customer ready to solve the problem or meet a goal, the salesperson can ...

Try his or her sales presentation.

This approach is extremely powerful. It allows the salesperson to focus on the primary concerns of the customer in a logical, sequential fashion. Customers also appreciate this approach as an effective means of solving their problems and fulfilling their goals. See page 45 for more details on the F.A.C.T. agenda.

Just the FACTs...

FIND. Use open-ended questions (see "Open and closed probes," page 46) until the customer's problem or goal (as it pertains to your product or service) becomes apparent. Provide support statements when problems arise that you do not want to pursue, so that the customer feels understood (for example, *"Yes, I can see why that would be a dilemma. What about when it comes to this particular area; what are your problems here?"*). Typically, you'll need between one and 10 questions to uncover the problem or goal. One of the most useful questions is: *"What is the biggest challenge in your area these days?"* This essentially directs the customer to the area of greatest concern, and can help to head off the customer's saying "I have no problem," since he or she is forced to identify a problem — hopefully, one you can solve. This line of thinking applies to goals as well.

Analyze. Once the problem or goal has been "found," use open-ended questions to uncover more details. For example, let's say you've identified a retail customer's problem as falling sales. Here you can learn more about the problem by asking about numbers of customers, store traffic, salespeople on the floor, and so on. This type of background information allows for a better understanding of the customer's problem and will facilitate a tailored solution.

CONSIDER consequences. Find a tactful — not too obvious or mundane — way of asking what happens if the problem is not solved or the goal is not met. This is typically a very challenging question for salespeople, and they often fail to ask it. Why? Sometimes they perceive it as being too obvious or aggressive. Here it's important to remember that the "consequences" question helps the customer to feel an emotional need to solve the problem. It is not intended to be asked in an obviously unattractive fashion. Some suggested approaches might be: *"Help me understand the implications of not hitting this goal on time"*; or, *"I imagine this is a pretty serious goal for your organization, given the time constraints"*; or, *"How bad is it?"*

TRY your sales presentation. Wrap up the question-asking process with your succinct and attractive description of what you have to offer the customer. (This process will be discussed in more detail later in the chapter.)

Open and closed probes

It is valuable to distinguish between two types of questions, or probes: open and closed. Open probes are intended to encourage the customer to open up or volunteer details not specifically requested. Closed probes are intended to solicit a specific (and usually brief) response such as *"Yes"* or *"No"* or *"Six."* Most salespeople believe themselves to be skilled at using open probes. However, we tend to use closed probes more often than we realize.

Try the following exercise, by yourself or with a friend. Use alternating open and closed probes in sequence. Start with an open probe such as *"How do you feel about . . .,"* then follow with a closed probe such as, *"Do you feel that is important?"* Next try another open probe, another closed probe, and so on.

Open probes are usually used to uncover a customer's beliefs, feelings, or information about his or her situation. Typically, you want to find out what it will take to satisfy a customer, to get the customer to expand on a line of thinking, or to open up a subject under discussion.

Closed probes are used when salespeople wish to verify that the information they possess is correct. They use closed questions to focus a line of thinking. Closed probes usually start with some form of the verb "to be" (is, are, were, isn't, etc.), "to do" (does, doesn't, don't), or "to have" (has, have, hadn't).

One type of open probe is called the *high-gain* question. It is intended to elicit a thoughtful response from the customer. Here, you ask the listener to elaborate on ideas and share his or her opinion. For example, the question *"What is your opinion of that?"* is generally very productive. It might build rapport because the person is allowed to pay tribute to himself or herself. It might uncover what it will take to get the customer to be supportive. It might even uncover valuable information about how others feel about a matter.

Piggy-backing your questions

As discussed earlier, we sometimes preface our questions with a support statement. Such statements are designed to help ensure the customer sees a rational flow to our line of thinking. This helps the customer feel comfortable about our intentions. Making these types of statements before asking questions is called *piggy-backing*.

An example of piggy-backing might be: *"That sounds like it is an important thing for us to discuss; tell me, how long has this problem been recurring?"* or, *"In our industry, failure rates are a major issue; what sort of rate have you been experiencing lately?"* (The support-statement part of the question is indicated with bold type.) Piggy-backing questions, such as those above, justify pursuing a particular line of reasoning. They make the customer recognize why you are asking a question, and they make the question appear less aggressive.

MAKING YOUR PRESENTATION

After uncovering a customer's primary goals or needs, who is involved in the decision-making process, the budgetary and timing issues involved, as well as the criteria involved in making a buying decision, you can proceed to make your presentation — essentially a series of statements that address the identified needs and goals. When salespeople make this series of statements, they sell the *advantages* or *benefits* of their products. We will examine presentation skills specifically in Chapter 5.

◖ Benefit selling

One way of describing benefit selling is to consider the process of buying a pair of pants in a store. Let's say that you walk into a retail store that sells blue jeans, and you see that they have your size on a particular shelf. Approaching that shelf and removing a pair of jeans, you notice the

> ### By děfǐnǐ'tion
>
> **Features**: The characteristics or traits of a particular product.
> **Benefits**: The advantages those traits offer to the customer.

manufacturer and say, *"Ah, my favourite brand; just what I was looking for."* At that moment, your perception of the value of those jeans has just increased.

In most people's minds there is a kind of scale that balances value against cost. The value of the jeans in this case has just risen; the cost is not an issue because you haven't looked at the price tag. After looking at the style of blue jeans you might say to yourself, *"Ahh, my favourite style; just the one I was looking for."* So you would have a still higher perception of value. Looking at the stitching and the quality of the manufacturing, the perceived value increases yet again. By now, your sense of the product's value has reached a level that it didn't have before you entered the store. Then comes the moment of truth. You look at the price tag and make a judgement — weighing the product's perceived value against its cost.

If the value perceived is greater than the cost, chances are you'll buy the product. If the value is less than the cost, you probably won't buy the product. And if they're the same? Chances are it will be the retail salesperson who influences your purchase.

It is up to salespeople to describe their products by focusing not so much on the features, but rather on the benefits offered to the customer. Benefits affect the value side of the equation; features do not.

On the other hand, it is important for the salesperson not to bore the customer by describing all the potential benefits of a particular product. Indeed, it is pertinent to describe only the benefits which apply to that particular customer. For example, let's say that you want to buy a new pen, and that you're interested in its appearance, comfort, and quality. In such a case, it won't make much sense for the salesperson to point out that it has a clip, and that the benefit of the clip is that the pen is less likely to be lost. That particular benefit might be relevant to some other customer, but not necessarily to you.

One of the most tangible features that you can offer to customers is the success that other customers have experienced in their relationship with you. By mentioning success stories, without revealing secrets, you send a very influential message.

HANDLING OBJECTIONS

So far, you've set the context for the meeting with your customer, established a rapport, asked questions to uncover needs and goals, and described your products or services to maximize the customer's perception of value. It is at this point that your customer may raise an objection or hurdle to your gaining the sale. Fortunately, there is a reliable protocol for responding to objections.

◼1 Show empathy

Your first step is to show a keen understanding of the customer's concern, demonstrating empathy for his or her point of view. Here it's important to acknowledge the customer's perspective — that you fully understand it and respect it. However, this effort to support the customer's perspective should not undermine your own point of view.

For example, if the customer's objection is, *"I've heard you guys are crooks,"* you're obviously not going to say, *"Yes, we are crooks; some of the worst around."* In this kind of situation, you should show empathy by agreeing with the customer's cause for concern. For example, you could say, *"Well, that's a very serious issue. I imagine if I thought a potential supplier were unethical, it would give me serious concern as well."* In this case, you have agreed in principle with the customer's concern, but not with the claim itself. This is very difficult for most salespeople, and severely tests their ability to balance empathy and focus. The natural temptation for most of us upon hearing an objection is to become defensive, to allow our egos to engage so that, rather than showing an understanding of the customer's concern, we wind up defending our positions and making the customer feel unheard.

2 Provide a new perspective

The second step in responding to a customer's objections is to provide the customer with a new point of view to consider. There are three alternative points of view you can try.

"IT'S ACTUALLY GOOD NEWS"

Here you can say that the issue about which the customer is concerned is essentially good news. This method of responding to objections is used only rarely. It is effective when the customer simply does not recognize that an apparently negative situation actually may have a silver lining. This message — "It's actually good news" — can be useful to explain value for money, or the value that has been delivered versus the price being charged.

"I CAN HANDLE THIS"

Another type of post-empathizing response to an objection is to point out a *solution* to the problem being raised. This is perhaps the most common response to an objection, although it requires that the salesperson be able to find solutions to the problems or issues at hand. This response sends the optimistic message "I can handle this."

"UNFORTUNATELY, THAT'S THE WAY IT IS"

A third way to meet objections (after your initial empathetic offering) is simply to remain firm. Sometimes you just can't bend; you may have to say, *"Yes, the objection is valid and I can understand why it is a concern, since the consequences of this problem may be x, y, and z. Unfortunately, there's nothing I can do about it — that's the way it is."* This type of response is common when customers raise issues about inflexible matters such as credit or pricing. The message sent is a polite *"tough."*

◾3 Be prepared

Perhaps the most effective way to meet objections is to have anticipated them before your client meeting. In this way you can prepare responses and deliver them with ease. Many successful sales organizations train their employees on the most common objections heard from their customers. This process serves two purposes: it provides the organization with an opportunity to make internal changes that resolve legitimate customer issues; and it prepares the sales force with viable answers.

◾4 No "buts"

Between the first step of showing empathy and the second step of providing a different or new perspective, many salespeople tend to use the word "but." For example, the customer might say, *"I feel that your price is too high,"* and your response might be: *"I know what you mean. Nowadays we all want to know that we're getting the best possible value for money, but I want you to know that our price reflects the quality of the product . . ."* Note that the salesperson has used the word "but" (as well as the "it's actually good news" answer).

Unfortunately, the word "but" sends a message to the customer that essentially says the equivalent of *"I didn't mean what I just said; I was only saying it to make you feel heard."* For this reason it often makes sense to replace "but" with "and." Initially, this may seem awkward, but over time you will discover the replacement word serves essentially the same purpose.

Grammatically, the word "but" is a disjunction, breaking apart two clauses; on the other hand, the word "and" is a conjunction which joins two ideas. Consequently, using "and" instead of "but" is less argumentative. Rather than contradicting the customer's perspective (and apparently trying to change it to your perspective), you are instead *adding* to the customer's point of view and, in a sense, broadening it to include your own.

This is another example of how consultative selling places a higher priority on the customer than on the salesperson.

CLOSING

At the end of every sales call, we try to close. This means attempting to gain the customer's commitment — either to buy or to undertake some next step. One rule of thumb when it comes to closing is: *"you must ask for commitment."*

Where the commitment is an agreement to take a next step, here's a second rule of thumb: the next step should be determined by the salesperson, *not* just the customer. The reason for this is perhaps obvious: it means that the customer is unable to procrastinate and that you are the one calling back, ready to move forward because of some accomplishment on your part.

Closing might simply be a request for another meeting, for permission to come back for a more thorough presentation, or for the invitation to submit a written quotation. When closing is seen in this light, it is less challenging for the salesperson and more fulfilling, as well. Of course, walking out of a customer's office with his or her agreement to consider a written presentation is very satisfying — if that was your desired result. But if your goal was actually to close the sale, then that same approval could be somewhat demoralizing.

As a compliance tactic, closing is very critical in the process of influencing a customer. Essentially, you want to make the closing question as clear as possible so that in the long run, customers do not waver in their commitments.

A customer who says, *"Sure, we'll give this serious consideration,"* has not necessarily agreed to a sale, even though you might return to your office proudly announcing your success. So you should make sure that you clarify the details of the customer's agreement so that he or she is more committed. For example, you could respond by asking more about what things might be considered and addressing those points individually; or you could say, *"Well, can I put in the order today so that you'll have it by next Tuesday?"* This effort to nail down the details of the commitment is very important to the selling process. Without it, an apparent sale can disappear in a puff of smoke.

In consultative selling, closing is meant to be a very natural process. This differs from the old-fashioned "hard sell," where closing is relatively awkward for both parties. In the consultative model, closing is a natural step in a logical questioning process. If rapport has been established and there is a sense of trust — and if the customer's need has been uncovered and it is clear that your product satisfies it — then logic dictates that the customer should agree to your proposal. More importantly, customers are increasingly driven to close when prices are desirable, real customer value is demonstrated, and all concerns have been addressed. When salespeople complete each of these tasks, the close becomes a sequential next step, as opposed to an awkward moment in the sale.

CLOSING METHODS
For over a century people have been writing books about various closing methods. One method involved closing one's brief case and approaching the exit so that the customer actually begs for the salesperson to stay.

Another method, known as the **puppy dog close**, has the salesperson prompting the customer to try the product for a while in order to establish commitment to using the product. This method causes the customer to commit, if only temporarily. But in short order the customer's self-image grows to accommodate permanent ownership. Consistency shifts into gear.

Another method is the **assumptive close**, whereby the salesperson asks, *"Do you want this product on Tuesday or Thursday?"* The intention here is to trick the customer. By choosing one of the two options presented, the customer is essentially choosing to buy.

And then there is the **Ben Franklin close**, where the salesperson draws a line down the middle of the page and walks the customer through what is supposed to be a logical analysis of the pros and cons of the purchase. The "logic" becomes skewed toward the salesperson's perspective, thereby influencing the customer's decision.

There are hundreds of closing methods. Some are deceitful and grossly manipulative — and, as such, have contributed to giving salespeople a bad name. In the consultative selling model, many of these methods are inappropriate, because consultative selling does not allow tricks of this nature to win business. Instead, consultative selling says that the customer will buy if he or she recognizes value and the sales-person has been effective in demonstrating that value. As long as the salesperson is focused, drives conversations towards goals, uncovers legitimate needs, provides a legitimate means of fulfilling those needs, stays professional, and remains highly empathetic, the sale will proceed naturally.

On the other hand, consultative selling does not mean you should be wishy-washy at the end of a business meeting. You must still be assertive. It is one thing not to be hard sell; it is another not to close. Even in a consultative mode, you always remember that, at the end of every sales meeting, you must gain commitment to the next step. The ball must

Build Commonality Before You Lead

Among all of the hundreds of techniques available to salespeople for clos-ing, the ultimate method can be expressed in one very simple principle: "Build commonality before you lead."

This simple five-word mission essentially summarizes consultative selling. It mandates the salesperson to build a warm bond with the customer, and to reach a point where the two parties are united in their recognition of what must be done and in their acceptance of a viable solution that brings true value at a very fair price. This mutual alignment then allows the salesperson to lead the customer towards the solution by virtue of his or her question-ing, benefit selling, objection handling, and ultimate closing gesture.

We follow the rule "build commonality before you lead" when we first establish a meeting. We don't drive a meeting forward until we have a sense of agreement or commonality in the room. We don't begin asking questions until a sense of rapport has been established. We don't move from asking questions to selling our ideas until we seem to have a sense of agreement of what the problems are and what the current situation is. We do not move from an objection to the close until we have the sense that there is a common agreement that the objection has been satisfacto-rily handled. And we don't move from the overall presentation to the close itself until we have the sense that the customer concurs that the product we are proposing, at the price we are suggesting, satisfies the desired requirements and yields sufficient value. The rule "build com-monality before you lead" goes to the very heart of consultative selling.

end up bouncing back into your court. Failure to gain this commitment means that you have ceased to be consultative — and have entered the realm of being just "too soft."

KEEPING THE SALE CLOSED

Once a sale has been secured, it is important for you to ensure that it remains a closed piece of business. You can undertake part of this task at the time of closing by ensuring that the customer's intention to buy a certain amount of product — for a certain number of dollars, on a certain day, and with certain other details well established — is as clear as possible. As discussed earlier in this chapter, a customer response of *"Yup, sounds good"* is often not enough; that's why it makes sense to review explicitly what has been agreed to.

Even after you've clarified all the details of the transaction, however, it is still possible for the customer to come down with a bad case of "buyer remorse." This term refers to the regret people sometimes feel after they have committed to a purchase — typically because, on reflection, they feel they have acted too swiftly, or could have negotiated a better price. You can go a long way towards heading off buyer remorse if, once the commitment has been made, you spend time talking with your customer about the intelligence of his or her decision.

After clarifying and firming up the commitment, it may be time to ask for referrals — the names and contact information of other people you might contact. (Depending on the circumstances, you may even be able to have the new customer make the contact on your behalf.) Another (and perhaps better) opportunity for requesting referrals might be when you follow up with the customer on a post-delivery quality control call.

SUMMARY

1. When salespeople meet with clients they generally follow a sequence of steps:
   - Introduce the meeting.
   - Build rapport.
   - Ask questions to uncover needs and opportunities.
   - Make their presentations.
   - Handle objections.
   - Close; obtain agreement to the next step.

   This is a logical process which requires the salesperson to be keenly focused and have special empathy skills.

2. *Rapport* comes from:

   - projecting *honesty;*
   - demonstrating *competence;*
   - showing *propriety;* and
   - building *commonality.*

   There are four different levels of commonality:
   - interests;
   - speech;
   - posture; and
   - thinking.

3. After introducing the meeting and establishing rapport, the salesperson begins to ask questions. During this phase of selling, focus on exactly what you can do for the customer, usually in terms of helping to solve a problem or reach a goal. You may have to gather some background information regarding timing of the project, decision makers, and the decision process. Also attempt to uncover budget information so that you know what funds are available.

4. One method by which salespeople follow a line of reasoning when questioning a customer is known by the acronym F.A.C.T. Here, the salesperson attempts to **Find** the problem, **Analyze** the nature of that problem, and ask the customer to **Consider** the consequences of the problem; thereafter, with the customer ready to solve the problem or meet a goal, the salesperson can **Try** his or her sales presentation.

5. Questioning techniques can include *open probes* (to get the customer to open up, or provide unsolicited detail), or *closed probes* (to confirm a point or drive the conversation in a different direction). You have to make sure the flow of the conversation is comfortable for the customer, so use support statements to *piggy-back* your questions as you go.

6. *Benefit selling* is the heart of the sales meeting. In a consultative context, you describe your solutions and the ways in which you can help clients reach goals. You attempt to distinguish yourself from other suppliers by pointing out the value that you can bring. You don't just describe *features* or characteristics of who you are and what you sell; doing so simply won't increase the customer's sense of *value*. Often salespeople assume, when they describe features, that the customer sees the logical benefit. That assumption is risky.

7. Once you have presented your products or services, the customer has an opportunity to voice his or her concerns, or *objections*. This is another challenge to your ability to balance empathy and focus. Use your empathy to ensure that the customer feels understood. Use your focus skills to paint a picture that satisfactorily addresses the customer's concerns. There are three types of available responses, summarized by the following phrases:

   - "It's actually good news..."
   - "I can handle this."
   - "Unfortunately, that's the way it is..."

8. *Closing* is the *natural* consequence of a consultative selling approach, and of having authentic value to bring to the table. When you have done your job well, this next step will follow — it does not require an aggressive, manipulative, or deceptive attempt to gain the customer's agreement. In the consultative model, closing still requires a certain level of assertiveness.

Presentation Skills

Sales presentations basically fall into two categories: the formal, *boardroom style* and informal, *sit-down style.*

Boardroom-style presentations generally involve speaking to groups in a formal environment, often with the presenter giving a prepared speech which calls upon various visual aids.

In this book, however, we'll be focusing on sit-down presentations, which are frequently just as important as their formal counterparts. They occur when a salesperson returns to a prospective customer's location to conduct a presentation which addresses that client's need. They usually occur after a preliminary meeting, in which there was a two-way conversation to build rapport and uncover needs, and which the salesperson closed with the intent of returning for another, more comprehensive presentation.

There are two principal elements of a presentation. The first is the actual *content* (or *meaning*) of the presentation. The second element is the *form* (or *style* or *method*) of delivery.

CONTENT

There are two fundamental requirements for the content of a sales presentation: *empathy* (building audience identification with you, your subject, and your propositions); and *focus* (using a logical, structured series of arguments).

◀ Empathy

The primary purpose of your presentation is to show people why they should buy into your ideas. You try to influence decisions and actions. One of the best ways to do this is by making your audience identify with what you have to say.

Audience identification occurs when the speaker is in touch with the mood, needs, and expectations of the audience. If the audience members can "see themselves" in the speaker and identify with the perspective and concepts of the presentation, then they will buy into the ideas. It is through the use of empathy that the speaker can achieve and maintain audience interest and identification, and give a persuasive presentation.

The rule "build commonality before you lead" reflects the key to effective presentations.

In Practice

The two presentations given below are distinct. While the message is the same, the audience is much more likely to identify with one of the presentations than with the other. Read both presentations to yourself; determine which of the two is the more attractive to you — and why.

Presentation 1

This book is designed to offer its readers valuable skills and information useful for their careers. To be successful, readers need only digest the material as it is presented and try their best to install their new understanding in their day-to-day lives. As a result, readers will derive significant benefit to their career development.

Presentation 2

In your job you need specific skills to be successful. This book is designed to give you those skills and other information that will be useful in your career. In order to be successful with this program, all you have to do is digest the material as presented and try as hard as you can to install the material in your day-to-day life. As a result, you will notice significant improvement in the progress of your career. Situations will arise where you struggle with ideas in this textbook. It is important that you understand that the solution to the problem is to slow down and read the troubling portion several times in order to digest its meaning. Doing so will help you to optimize the value you derive from the program.

Questions

1. Which of the two presentations is more attractive?

2. How many times did the word "you" appear in Presentation 2?

3. What is the effect of warning the customer of various challenges that will be faced as he or she attempts to utilize or take advantage of your product?

In order to use your empathy skills to build audience identification, it is important to consider a number of questions in advance of your presentation. Examples of such questions are shown in the "Personal Check" box at right.

Each of your answers to these questions will help you to tailor your presentation directly to your audience. So if you know what will please the audience, it may be important to mention that up front. If you can anticipate the key concern, you will be able to address it in your presentation. By establishing what you have in common with the audience, you can start your presentation with reference to that commonality in order to optimize rapport. Ultimately, it's a matter of knowing what your listeners need to hear from you in order to reach your goal, and then telling it to them.

Consultative presentation skills require a high level of audience identification, partially because this is what customers expect. They expect someone to talk about them. They expect someone to address their needs. They expect someone to behave in a manner that matches their idea of how a supplier should behave. In this sense, the answer to the question *"What is the key to conducting a winning sales presentation?"* is profoundly simple: **the customer!**

Using empathy to build audience identification involves simple things such as using the word *"you"* or starting your presentation with remarks that demonstrate your understanding of how the audience feels, such as: *"Thank you for giving me your time today—I know you are busy."* It also involves trying to anticipate the audience's unspoken ideas

---

☑ *Personal Check*

Understanding your audience

☐ How many people will be present, and what time of day will it be?

☐ Will the final decision-makers be present?

☐ Will the key members of the audience be ready to make final decisions?

☐ Can they afford my fee or price or program or terms?

☐ What will be the age and sex of the audience?

☐ What will excite or please them?

☐ What will be their key concern?

☐ What problem or issue do they need to solve?

☐ Whom do they respect or report to?

☐ Whose opinion will be influential?

☐ What sort of information will they want or expect from me?

☐ What do they know or assume about me?

☐ What do I have in common with the audience?

☐ What sort of style, format, or setup will the audience or situation dictate?

☐ Are there any hidden or problem issues that will need special handling?

☐ Can I ask for the order?

☐ What is the organization's political, social, and economic climate?

☐ What will they need to hear from me in order for me to reach my goal?

☐ What will be the physical environment for my presentation?

concerning your remarks. This empathetic effort to know what people are thinking allows you to address — and affirm — their views.

In the same way, it is valuable for you to talk less about yourself (or your organization or product or ideas) and more about the audience. This may be as simple as changing your grammatical approach, resisting the temptation to use the word "I" as the subject of your sentences. For example, rather than saying, *"I want you to know ...,"* try saying *"You may be interested to know...."*

◀■ Focus

In addition to building audience identification, sales presentations have to prove a point or cause some specific effect. This proof is generally accomplished by presenting data and providing an interpretation of those data. These modes of presentation are called, respectively, the *data dump* and *logical argumentation.*

Data dump. In this type of presentation you simply list all the reasons that you think your company and its products are special — often as a series of bullet points. It's a fairly common approach to presentations — unfortunately, it is inconsistent with the idea of consultative benefit selling that we've been developing in this book.

Logical argumentation. This presentation style, which shows the logic of your proposition, is usually more effective than the data dump method. For example, rather than listing only features and benefits, it may be more advantageous to show how your company and its products can meet the specific goal of the prospect better than any other company. Then it will logically follow that the customer should buy from you. The information from the data dump still goes into the presentation, but it is provided in a context.

A data dump leaves the thinking to the listeners, while the logical argumentation makes the presentation more persuasive. So, given that a presentation is intended to influence people rather than just to share information, it helps to be logical, clear and to the point. It helps to make your primary point perfectly clear.

USING STRUCTURE TO ENHANCE FOCUS

A focused presentation should follow some sort of logical agenda. An agenda is a series of steps in a process. A common agenda for a presentation prescribes three main steps: opening; body; and closing.

In Practice

Consider the two presentations shown below. Which would you describe as a data dump? Which one attempts to build an argument?

Presentation 1

We offer reduced waste, the best yield, and a long product life. We pride ourselves on our fast delivery, twenty-four hour service, and two-year guarantee.

Presentation 2

You indicated that your goal was to find the best supplier — one who will make you optimum profit and minimize your headaches. We will make you optimum profit because we offer reduced waste, best yield, and a long product life. We will save you headaches because we offer fast delivery, 24-hour service and a two-year guarantee. Therefore, we are your best supplier, offering you optimum profit and minimum headaches.

While the information given in both presentations is essentially the same, the second presenter incorporated material that the first presenter assumed was obvious to the audience.

Note, too, how the second presentation appears to be more focused. By painting a very clear picture of your logic, you will be more influential to your audience. (Recall what we said in Chapter 2 about using reason as a compliance tactic.)

Of course, the opening-body-closing structure is only a shell. The body portion actually contains your logical argument. And your argument will most often have the data structured in a certain order — structure within structure within structure. People like structure. We organize ideas in various ways to help us understand them. Here are some other structures:

- *chronological* (past, present, future);
- *sequential* (first, second, third);
- *geographical* (north, south, east, west);
- *categorical* (apples, oranges, bananas, or triangles, circles, squares);
- *hierarchical* (top, middle, bottom);
- *goal-oriented* (problem, alternatives, solution).

Order improves understanding. In fact, telling people what order you are going to use before you use it improves understanding even more. The idea is to avoid throwing ideas out randomly, or doing a data dump. Your argument must be structured, consisting of three parts: the opening, the body, and the closing.

Referring back to the "In Practice" box on the previous page, note how a logical presentation gets assembled in Presentation 2. In this case, the presenter had a point to prove — that he or she had exactly what the customer wanted — and offered a three-part argument: the customer wanted optimal profit and minimal aggravation; the presenter offered optimal profit; and the presenter offered minimal aggravation. This argument, if accepted, essentially forces the conclusion. To support the argument, the presenter offered (organized) supporting data as evidence (reduced waste, best yield, etc.) — all within a structure.

FORM

Once the content of your presentation is organized, it is time to think of your intended *form* or *delivery style*. Here you want to keep your audience attentive, intrigued, and feeling good about you. As mentioned earlier, this can be accomplished through building rapport. The challenge for many presenters is to keep the audience attentive and focused on the ideas being presented.

People usually speak at a rate of about 150 words a minute. However, we *think* at a rate of approximately 450 words a minute. Within this discrepancy, a listener's thoughts can easily wander from what is being said.

◼ Scoring hits

In order to grab the audience's attention so that everyone's thoughts remain with your presentation, you need to employ a series of "hits" — usually at intervals of 30 to 60 seconds. Typical "hits" include:

- pauses;
- using vocal skills such as tonal variation and inflection changes;
- humour and other sources of entertainment;
- hand gestures;
- posture changes;
- using the term "You";
- reminding the audience of your main point; and
- visual aids.

Even for informal, sit-down presentations, hits are important.

VOCAL SKILLS

Vocal skills are particularly critical. Indeed, effective presenters often seem to be able to communicate messages by inflection alone.

Some speech coaches suggest rehearsing speeches repeatedly in order to master your inflection. This allows you to direct your mental energies to the expression of the words rather than the words themselves.

Good presenters know their material well and are believable as a result. The message here is simple — practise, practise, practise.

Try the exercises below to test the control you have over your inflection. If possible, ask a friend to listen and determine whether you are successful in conveying the meanings you intend.

☑ *Personal Check*

Developing vocal skills

☐ Use repeated rehearsal to burn new pathways in the brain.

☐ Tape yourself, or get a friend to practise with you to provide feedback.

☐ Like an actor, learn to convey emotions — it will make your presentations more expressive.

In Practice

1. Consider the statement *I did not say, "He drives too fast."* On which word would you place spoken emphasis to convey the following meanings?
   - Running was the issue; not driving.
   - Your concern was with his being too slow.
   - You believe that someone else made the statement.
   - You never really thought that it was too fast in the first place.
   - It was Frank who drove too fast; not Andy.
   - You only implied that you were concerned with the speed.

2. Read aloud the statement *I said, "I hate role-playing."* Now read the following variations, placing emphasis on the bold italicized words. What different meanings are conveyed?
   - *I* said, "I hate role-playing."
   - I *said,* "I hate role-playing."
   - I said, "*I* hate role-playing."
   - I said, "I *hate* role-playing."
   - I said, "I hate *role-playing.*"

Handling a Nervous Voice

Your voice reflects your self-confidence. If your voice sounds thin or wavering, nervousness may be affecting your breathing. Try placing your hand over your heart and making the sound come from that area. Try breathing not from your chest cavity, but from your diaphragm.

VISUAL AIDS

Used properly, visual aids can be very helpful during informal presentations. They serve a variety of purposes, such as

- Focusing attention on what is being discussed by having participants visually review the material.
- Increasing interest in the topic being discussed by presenting material that is visually appealing.
- Enhancing retention by engaging more than one sense (hearing and seeing) in the presentation of the material.

☑ *Personal Check*

Steadying your nerves

☐ Know your material well.

☐ Practise at home — out loud.

☐ Pamper yourself.

☐ Recognize that your nervousness is an asset — it makes you try your best and can give you tremendous focus.

While visual aids can help to keep listeners attentive, there is a danger: if the audience becomes overly focused on the visual aids, they may lose track of your message. To avoid this possibility, direct your audience's attention — either by literally pointing to the item if the situation allows, or by referring to a specific spot in the visual aid. (For example, *"Let me draw your attention to the second last paragraph where it says…"*)

If the visual aid is in the form of a handout, be sure to

- Title the handout.
- Identify the purpose of the handout.
- Specify when and how the handout is to be used.
- Reference any additional materials needed to use it.
- Use attractive typesetting and fonts, with bold print, underlining, or capitals, as appropriate.
- Space information so it is easily read.
- Use short, active (not passive) sentences.

- Avoid unnecessary information.
- Ensure that your written handouts are perfect in all respects. Eliminate spelling errors, typographical errors, and even signs of poor photocopying.

As a rule of thumb, don't hand out handwritten documents. Even if your customers are used to informality, a competitor could step in with a more professional presentation and steal what you believed to be guaranteed business, simply by virtue of having created a perception of superior credibility.

Regardless of whether the document is a handout for a presentation or a quick quotation, it should be perfect and impeccably professional. In any written material you produce, there is no room for errors in spelling or grammar, photocopier toner stains, or crumpled paper.

SUMMARY

1. Most sales presentations are not to large audiences; more often they're informal, sit-down pitches designed to present the big picture of a potential business relationship.

2. There are two primary things to consider when preparing a sales presentation: *content* and *form*. Content concerns what is said and how it is organized. Form concerns our style of delivery.

3. Content can be broken down into two main sub-components: *empathy* and *focus*. Empathy, in the context of a sales presentation, is the ability to make your listeners identify with your message because you are accurately addressing their unspoken thoughts. Focus reflects your logical presentation of ideas in a way that makes your content easy to understand and attractive to accept. Empathy and focus are recurring themes for sales success: how well you address where the customer is coming from and how well you stay on track with your own goals.

4. Form involves keeping an audience attentive to your message. This can be accomplished with "hits," which include pauses and changes in tone and inflection.

5. Visual aids, properly used, can also be useful for sustaining an audience's interest. Such aids may include printed handouts, and they must be highly professional in appearance.

6. Nervousness can be controlled by knowing your material well, and rehearsing your presentation repeatedly. Breathing practice can help develop a strong, confident voice.

Negotiation Skills

Sooner or later, every sale comes down to a series of discussions that finalize the deal. The issues to be resolved may include final pricing or other terms. But in all cases both the salesperson and the customer want to move forward. This is the point where your negotiation skills come to the fore.

RESOLVING CONFLICT

Conflict or disagreement should not be perceived as a test of power or a sign of failure, but rather as an opportunity to reveal what people need. This will ultimately lead to areas of agreement or compromise.

Eventually, one party will move towards compromise. Negotiators should listen carefully for signs that indicate an attempt to compromise is being offered. Statements beginning with *"suppose that"* or *"what if"* or *"how would you feel about"* are indicators that compromise is near.

When responding to offers, it is a good practice to restate them. For example, *"You will give me A, B, and C for D dollars less than the retail price?"*

However, even before arriving at a compromise there are a number of basic rules of thumb to keep in mind if you want to steer your negotiations towards a mutually satisfying outcome.

1 Listen closely

Success in negotiation does not come from being all focus and no empathy. A lack of basic listening skills and compassion can lead to buyer remorse, lost future business, and unsuccessful negotiations. In fact, acute empathy skills help to define exactly what another party needs in order finally to close a deal.

◀2 Know where you want to go

Successful negotiators plan what they will ask for and how much they are willing to bend. They predict the moves or tactics of their opponents and they formulate defensive countermeasures in advance.

◀3 Aim high

If you aim higher, you'll achieve higher. When you are in a negotiation, don't be afraid to offer low on the buying side and ask high on the selling side. Be careful, however, that you don't ask for too much. If you do, a reverse version of reciprocity can kick in; the other party may simply get offended and want to quit negotiating.

◀4 Consider deadlines

People often wait until deadlines approach before they settle a negotiation. Therefore, be aware of your deadlines — and those of your counterpart. Using this information effectively can be of significant benefit. For example, it is valuable to know your customer's deadlines so that you can predict when he or she will move towards compromise — which is usually just before it's too late. Conversely, understand how your customer's knowledge of your own deadlines can be used as a tool to stall negotiations until you are in a panic.

◀5 Don't be afraid of deadlock — when appropriate

People have an inherent need for closure. They don't like to start something and walk away without results. This part of our psyche can cause negotiators to make concessions or bad decisions, just to avoid deadlock. Successful negotiators know when deadlock is acceptable and they are not afraid of it.

◀6 Use a cooperative approach for win–win results

Don't think of negotiations as a battle to be won, where your opponent must be conquered. Successful negotiators treat their counterparts with respect and look for ways to achieve a deal that will satisfy both parties. By working together, two parties can achieve a better deal than if they are working at cross-purposes.

▃7 Look for a better deal

There is often a better deal available for both parties, and successful negotiators are always looking for it. Therefore, once both parties are in agreement, they pause to examine the ways in which the deal could be improved for both sides.

▃8 Don't talk too much

Successful negotiators don't talk — they ask questions. The more you talk, the more information you give to your counterpart.

▃9 Resist concessions

In the give-and-take process of negotiation, the "gives" are called concessions. The ultimate goal is to achieve a mutually beneficial agreement where you grant a relatively small number of concessions. Several experiments in the area of negotiation and influence suggest that negotiators who give concessions reluctantly and in small amounts tend to be more successful.

▃10 Allow your opponent to save face

If you've given your opponent your absolute best offer, and he or she claims to have given you the same, there will be a natural reluctance for the other party to yield, since this will make his or her claim appear inconsistent. Here you can offer some unrelated, secondary concession, in order to allow him or her to bend without appearing to do so.

▃11 Remember your compliance tactics

The various compliance tactics discussed in previous chapters all come into play during negotiations. For example, you use *authority* when you back up claims with proven information or when you have to talk to your boss to get various approvals. Deadlines represent a *scarcity* of time. *Reciprocity* applies to handling concessions: if your opponent asks for something, you can expect him or her to respond positively to your request for some concession in return. *Consistency* applies in the previous rule about saving face. The tendency to behave consistently with what you have said actually necessitates the use of reciprocity to allow the opposition to bend without looking inconsistent.

▬12 Don't be victimized by others' compliance tactics

Making compliance theory work for you is good, but you must also be able to recognize when it is being used by the other party. For example, if you are negotiating with a very senior member of a customer's organization — someone who represents *authority* — you may be inclined to offer more than you might with a more junior person. On the other hand, you may feel unnecessarily pressured by the principle of *reciprocity* to offer something in return for an opponent's concession when, in fact, you could simply stand firm.

SUMMARY

1. When the customer is ready to move forward but wants to get improved pricing and/or other arrangements, negotiations begin.

2. Successful negotiators adhere to a number of simple rules of thumb. These include:

   • Aim high so there is room to move.
   • Don't be afraid of deadlock.
   • Know in advance how low you are willing to go, or you could end up with "seller remorse."
   • Let your counterparts back out of claims that they have given you their "best" offer; use reciprocity, offering one more (inconsequential) concessions so that they can respond in kind.

3. All of the compliance tactics discussed so far in this book are used when we negotiate. *Scarcity* of time can make you panic, so don't let it get to you. *Authority* may intimidate you, so stay level-headed. *Reciprocity*, when used by the counterpart, involves offering a concession, but only in exchange for something else. *Consistency* shows up in many ways: it can work against you (for example, if you offer something, it must stay on the table) or it can work in your favour (for example, if a customer wants to negotiate, it means that the customer's self-image is consistent with a purchase from you; it means they want things to work).

Review: Tactical selling skills

1. Compliance theory applies to the real world of interactive selling. It employs human tendencies to respond to certain stimuli in more or less predictable ways. This necessarily raises ethical questions — questions that can be resolved if a salesperson always remembers the principles of *"don't deceive"* and *"bring value for money."*

2. Sales success also depends on balancing *empathy* and *focus*. Another recurring prescription is *"Build commonality before you lead."* (In Part 3, we'll be looking at how empathy requires self-restraint or ego management.)

3. Tactically, *empathy* requires an authentic investment in the customer. The salesperson makes an effort to hear the customer and demonstrates what has been heard through the use of tactics like validating objections, making support statements, creating audience identification, and building commonality. Even attending to customer problems and opportunities is essentially an empathetic gesture, since it requires a temporary resignation of self while seeing another world view.

4. A form of goal-orientation, *focus* refers to defining the customer's situation, as well as driving conversation while using empathy to sustain the tacit permission. In the context of presenting a solution or idea, focus is used to organize and express your thoughts in a logically structured argument, thereby eliciting compliance via *reason*.

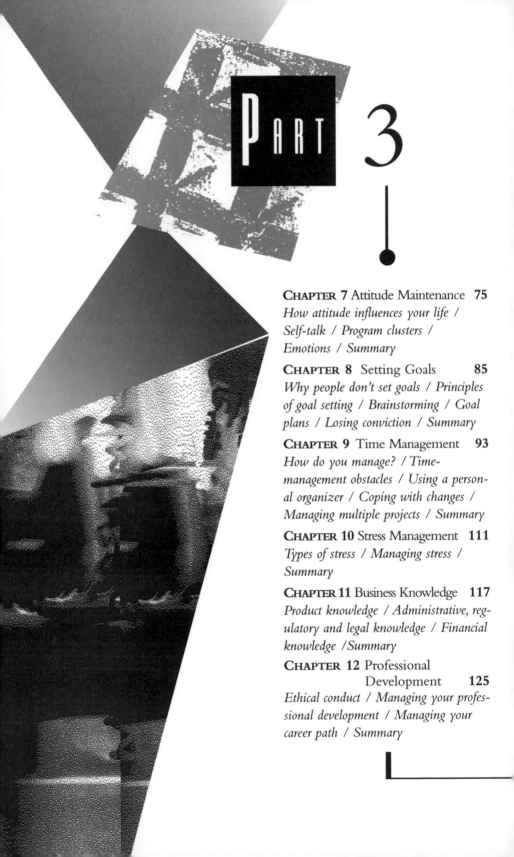

PART 3

SELF-MANAGEMENT SKILLS

In this section we'll be looking at how you can manage and develop the essential personality traits that lead to sales success.

Think of all the successful people you know and chances are they have one thing in common — they're remarkably effective at managing themselves, their thoughts, and their emotions. These are the people who seem to get more done than humanly possible. They never seem stressed. Everyone likes them — they always have a great attitude. They are exceedingly professional. They always seem to be setting and meeting goals. And even though they are empathetic and pleasant, they still seem always to be focused on the issues at hand.

In the following chapters we will examine five areas relating to self-management. Each one will provide you with some insight into yourself and your habits. You will learn about specific skills and techniques that can be used to improve your performance in each area. And ultimately, you will be prepared to become more like the super-successful people we just described.

Sales professionals require a common set of skills, traits, attitudes, and knowledge in order to be successful — regardless of the industry in which they work. So let's look at some of these factors in detail.

Attitude Maintenance

Attitude is our mental position about facts — or, more simply, the way we view things. How often have you heard someone say, *"He has a bad attitude"* or *"He has the **right** attitude"*? We know instinctively that attitude contributes to our success, and we instantly recognize the "right" and "wrong" attitude.

The way we look at the world has a powerful influence on our lives. There is a popular expression in advertising and marketing that states, "Perception is greater than reality." And it's true — how we perceive the world is what creates our individual reality.

How we view the world affects our lives in many ways: our health, our professional success, and our level of satisfaction with life. The good news is that our mental position about the world around us can be managed and maintained. We can control how we view the world. We can create a positive view that supports a successful life.

HOW ATTITUDE INFLUENCES YOUR LIFE

How does attitude influence our lives — and our success? Here are seven important points to consider:

1. **Your attitude towards people influences your behaviour towards them.** You can't always hide the way you feel. When people perceive you have a negative attitude towards them, it can make them defensive, or cause them to deflect their thoughts away from you. Prompting this type of response from customers is counterproductive to your role as a consultative salesperson.

2. **Your attitude affects your level of satisfaction with life, and with your job.** Your perception of the world translates into reality. If you perceive your life in a positive way, your life *will* be positive.

3. **Your attitude affects everyone who comes in contact with you, either in person or on the telephone.**

4. **Your attitude is reflected by your tone of voice, your posture, and your facial expression.** Because of this, it is extremely difficult, if not impossible, for you to prevent transmitting your attitude in everything that you do.

5. **Your attitude can affect your health.** There is ample medical evidence to prove that a poor or negative attitude can depress your immune system. People with depressed immune systems catch more colds and viruses, and are generally more susceptible to illness.

6. **A positive attitude can help you live longer.** Studies show that positive imaging works as an effective support to conventional cancer treatments. The right attitude may improve chances for recovery.

7. **Your attitude is not fixed.** Your attitude is up to you.

Quotable...

"As a person thinketh...so are they."

– JAMES ALLEN
Your Attitude Determines
Your Altitude. 1992

People who project enthusiasm and a positive attitude generally provide higher levels of customer service, and are more successful in all areas of their lives. So it only makes sense to maintain as positive an attitude as possible. Unfortunately, maintaining a positive attitude is not so easy.

Given that attitude is so important, we must ask ourselves: Where does attitude come from? *Can* we control our attitude? *Should* we control our attitude? And if so, how?

SELF-TALK

What is self-talk? It is simply the way in which you describe to yourself the world around you. Much of the time we are not aware of our self-talk; because we are so accustomed to it, it has become subconscious. In order to control self-talk, we need to understand how it works.

At every waking moment your mind is busy. When you perceive an event in the external world, your brain quickly searches through its vaults of previous experiences for every scrap of relevant information. In a split second it retrieves any previously programmed mental or behavioural responses. Based on those previous responses, you may jump for joy, feel depressed, start to laugh, lose your temper, run away, or simply have no reaction at all.

When your brain is chattering away to itself — that is, when it is simply generating thoughts without controlling them — those thoughts are primarily a result of our past experiences. The content or message being mulled over is pretty much a replay of "programs" stored in our bio-computer.

These programs — more technically described as "habituated points of view" — serve a critical purpose. They trigger our protective instincts for self-preservation or survival. They enable us to rationalize situations by relating our current experience to similar experiences in the past. Finally, they provide a kind of psychological buffer, relating new, stressful situations to experiences that we have dealt with in the past.

These programs often operate without our being directly aware of them. If we are actively doing something unrelated to the programs, for example, the thoughts generated by those programs are relegated to the periphery of our consciousness. The thoughts are available to us, but only if we pay attention to them. Either way, these programs cause us to interpret situations in a certain way — they generate our *self-talk*.

While we may not be conscious of it, our self-talk determines our behaviour. And if our behaviour does not correspond to our rational and conscious goals, we need to change the self-talk that is driving that behaviour. We can break out of our old routines and comfort zones, and create new ways of approaching experiences and situations that, reason tells us, have not been successful in the past. The important thing to remember is that our programs can be changed.

The attitude we project comes from our self-talk. We know that our self-talk comes from our lifetime of experience. And we know that self-talk can be changed. But how? First, we must become aware of our self-talk. To help you do this, complete the "In Practice" exercise on the following page.

Identifying negative self-talk

We add fuel to our belief systems by using the same self-talk over and over again. We use words to describe our attitude or situation that affect

In Practice

Do you recognize your own negative self-talk? Make a list of at least five "negative" self-talk phrases that you have used and could be affecting your level of sales performance. Examples are shown below.

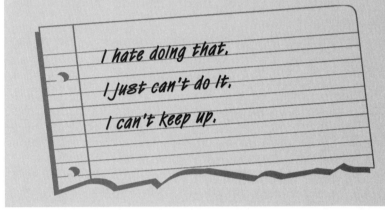

I hate doing that.

I just can't do it.

I can't keep up.

our outcomes. By changing the way we describe things to ourselves, we can change our attitude towards them. Consider the following phrases.

I CANNOT . . .

In most cases, "cannot" statements are untrue. To change a belief like this, start repeating to yourself that you *can* achieve your goal. For instance, if you say *"I can do arithmetic"* or *"I can sleep"* or *"I can lose weight"* you have a much better chance of meeting each of those objectives. The more you tell yourself that you can do something, the more likely it is that you will do it successfully.

I HAVE TO, OR I NEED TO . . .

There is very little that we actually have to do or need to do. We do not *have* to get up in the morning. We do not *need* to succeed. We do not *have* to eat. Everything, even living, is an option for us. Once we realize that we have options, that we *choose* to do things, a burden is lifted. We have power to do what we want to do. To begin new beliefs, use phrases such as *"I choose to exercise"* or *"I choose to work."*

SHOULD . . .

When we encounter a situation that makes us frustrated and angry, we often react against it with the word "should." For example, if all the telephones are busy, we think, *"This company* **should** *get a new system."* Or, if traffic is slow, we think, *"People* **should** *speed up."* Each time we make one of these statements, we tend to be feeling angry.

Such responses can be very energy-depleting. To overcome this habit, try to view frustrating occurrences more scientifically. Rational analysis will reveal that any given event is the product of a particular set of conditions. Whatever happened, simply happened. Once we begin to see events in this way, we no longer feel anger.

WHAT IF . . .

This phrase causes worry. It also depletes our energy. In fact, after a few "what if..." statements, we can actually begin to believe that what we are worrying about has already happened. Instead, consider the actual consequences of your "what if..." statement coming true. What is the worst possible scenario? Approached rationally, you will see that no situation is irrecoverable.

In Practice

Negative self-talk affects our attitude, which affects the outcome of our experiences. Learn to recognize negative self-talk, and discipline yourself to use positive self-talk to alter your pattern. Here's how you can begin this process.

Select three of the "negative" self-talk phrases that you listed in the "In Practice" exercise on page 78, then create a positive self-talk phrase for each. An example of this procedure is shown below.

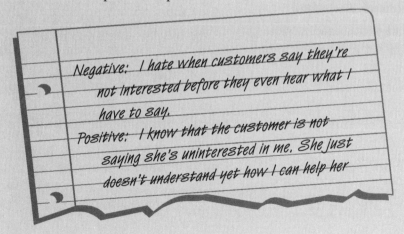

Negative: I hate when customers say they're not interested before they even hear what I have to say.

Positive: I know that the customer is not saying she's uninterested in me. She just doesn't understand yet how I can help her

... NEVER ...

... ALWAYS ...

EVERYBODY'S LIKE THAT ...

All three of these phrases are generalizations. They are seldom true and can cause us to become irrational, reaching conclusions that are equally false. For example, it's simply not accurate to say, *"These things never work out for me — I'll never close another sale."* Of course you will close another sale. This type of generalization can lead to the development of a pessimistic attitude and poor performance. It is exhibiting victim behaviour rather than agent behaviour.

IT'S NOT MY FAULT ...

This phrase is another indicator of victim-like thinking. It indicates that we are placing too much emphasis on avoiding blame, rather than being agents and dealing with the situation effectively.

█ Gaining control of self-talk

Directing our self-talk in a positive way is a key factor in maintaining a winning attitude. But how do we gain control of our self-talk?

The first step is to become aware of self-talk. Most of our self-talk is so unconscious, or habituated, that we are no longer aware of it. When you are dealing with a situation, or customer, discipline yourself to tune in to your self-talk. What are you telling yourself about the situation? What are your internal responses? With practice, you will come to know your self-talk in different situations.

In all situations, set your frame of mind in a positive attitude. When you become aware of negative self-talk, turn it around. (See "In Practice" on page 79.) Write down examples of positive self-talk which relate to stressful situations you encounter often. Refer to your list, practising the self-talk until it has become a new habituated point of view.

☑ *Personal Check*

Self-talk control techniques

☐ Develop awareness of your self-talk in different situations and with different people.

☐ Prepare for situations where your habituated point of view is negative by creating positive self-talk. Write them down and refer to the list often.

☐ Discipline yourself to use the positive self-talk you have created.

Prepare yourself for negative feedback from customers, employers, and others, and use the information to create positive results. Develop innovative techniques that work for you in turning negative self-talk into positive self-talk, and generate your own system for creative and positive thinking. Become an agent, not a victim.

PROGRAM CLUSTERS

Often our programmed attitudes, beliefs, and reactions are somewhat more complex than simple phrases or perspectives. They seem to have personalities of their own. This is because they are a result of related, deeply ingrained patterns of thinking. They are clusters of self-talk phrases, or *program clusters*.

For example, you might have a part of yourself that tends to be insecure, while having another part that tends to be outgoing and dynamic. Each of the parts seems to have its own personality. Some

In Practice

Here's an opportunity to identify the clusters of self-talk that make up your sub-personalities, and to determine whether they support or hinder your outcomes.

First, give names to some of your sub-personalities (for example, *fearful, low self-esteem, confident, enthusiastic*) and write them down, along with a brief description of each.

Now recall a situation where each identified sub-personality has surfaced. Was the outcome positive or negative?

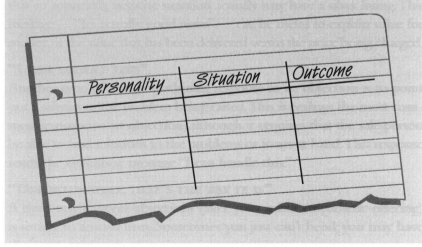

Personality	Situation	Outcome

psychologists refer to these complex patterns of behaviour as *sub-per-sonalities*. The field of psychology called psychosynthesis deals with sub-personalities.

Sometimes we give names to these sub-personalities in order to facilitate our understanding of their patterns of behaviour, thereby allowing us to recognize them when they are active. One might say, for example, *"I'm in my frightened 'little girl' right now,"* meaning that *"I am identifying with that part of me that manifests the programmed behaviour of a frightened little girl."*

On any given day, you might move several times from one sub-personality to another. There is nothing wrong with this, as long as there is some sense of balance or cooperation between various sub-personalities. Sometimes we can be over-identified with a particular part of ourselves, so that we get caught up in a mood, emotion, or point of view that is detrimental to our goals or success. This is the point where self-talk is most negative.

These program clusters relate directly to our patterns for success and failure. Recognizing the clusters of negative self-talk we use helps us to recognize our "failure patterns."

Take the time to determine the sub-personality you used in situations which did not work out for you. Learn to recognize such patterns, and discipline yourself to use positive self-talk to alter them.

EMOTIONS

Most of us have encountered situations that have caused us to react emotionally. The way we feel about something or someone affects our behaviour. Sometimes these emotions can actually hurt our chances of reaching our desired goals. If a situation arises which makes us angry, for example, we may react to our anger rather than remaining focused on our goal.

By gaining control over your emotions, you can improve your chances for success. That doesn't mean blocking them out or ignoring them. It just means having the ability to prevent emotions from determining behaviour. It means being in control of the things that are said and done at all times. Successful people don't react to their emotions; they recognize them, understand them, and deal with them.

Our emotions affect our self-talk. Therefore, the key to managing our emotional reactions is the effective use of positive self-talk.

Tips for Attitude Maintenance

Maintaining a positive, healthy, focused attitude is essential to achieving success — not just in our careers, but in all aspects of our lives. The following are some tips and reminders about how to maintain a positive attitude.

- **Be aware of self-talk.** Use this awareness to break out of routines and old habits that produce negative results. Understand that breaking these routines can remove you from your "comfort zone"; however it will also lead you towards new, more positive and productive patterns of self-talk.

- **Develop new techniques for approaching situations.** Don't confine yourself to your old styles of thinking and familiar routines. Be creative.

- **Plan ahead.** Anticipate situations and create positive self-talk to turn them around. Write down your results. Visualize your positive performance, and refer to your written notes often.

- **Teach yourself to recognize your positive and negative sub-personalities, or clusters of self-talk.** Create strategies to gain control of your patterns for success and failure. Practise self-discipline in managing your self-talk.

- **Place yourself in a positive environment.** Try to avoid situations that surround you with negative people or self-talk. Look for environments with positive people. Keep and refer to evidence of your past successes (such as awards or letters of commendation). Support your positive attitude by reading inspirational books, or listening to inspirational tapes.

SUMMARY

1. It is essential to maintain a positive attitude in any work environment — and especially so for sales professionals.

2. Self-talk has a profound effect on your attitude. There are a number of techniques for gaining a better understanding of your own self-

talk — particularly negative self-talk. This allows you to develop specific strategies for managing self-talk that will help you maintain a positive attitude on the job, thus maximizing sales performance.

Setting Goals

Successful people use set goals as a way to direct their energy, as well as to make and fulfill commitments in their personal and professional lives. These individuals have clearly-defined goals, which are kept in mind at all times. Goal-oriented people have realistic goals and concrete plans for achieving them. They write their goals down, and can articulate them clearly. Goal-oriented people often share their goals with the people around them, thereby gaining resources and support.

Goal setting can be used to define your personal vision, and to review how that vision aligns with and supports your organization's vision. This allows you to identify any conflict between personal and professional values and to develop plans to resolve such conflicts.

It is important to set specific long- and short-term goals to focus your efforts. Indeed, unless we set and actively pursue our goals, our success is left in the hands of others. This chapter will help in the process of identifying goals and creating a five-year plan for yourself.

WHY PEOPLE DON'T SET GOALS

Many people believe that goal setting doesn't really work. They are skeptical about the importance of goals and about the influence they have in determining future outcomes. These people generally consider themselves pawns in the game of life. They feel that success is determined by factors beyond their control. So they are content to wait for opportunity to knock on the door — or to pass them by. They are victims, not agents.

In some cases, people won't set goals because they are afraid to commit themselves. They are content to talk about their untapped potential instead of using it. People who don't believe in themselves don't set goals. They lack confidence, so they avoid situations where they might fail. Their approach can be summed up as *"If I don't try, I can't fail."*

Some people simply don't take the time to set goals. The average person spends more time planning a trip to the store than planning for success in the coming years. These people have never developed the discipline of focusing on what is really most important to them.

Another reason for not setting goals is that many people don't know how. This becomes a self-imposed barrier to their success. And some people do know how to set goals, but don't because they have never successfully achieved the goals that they have set previously. What is unfortunate about this group of people is that they probably could have avoided failure.

Unattainable Goals

Why do so many people fail to achieve their goals? Here are five of the main causes — causes that you can avoid.

1. **No chance.** If goals are unrealistic, you're bound to fail.

2. **No focus.** If you set too many goals, or if the goals are too vague, they'll be hard to achieve.

3. **No motivation.** Goals must be challenging or inspiring; if they're not, why bother?

4. **No plan.** Many people fail because they don't know how to reach their goals.

5. **No persistence.** You need a mechanism to help you maintain your conviction to achieve your goals.

PRINCIPLES OF GOAL SETTING

Here are a nine principles that can guide us in setting appropriate and attainable goals. Let's examine each of them.

◄1 Goal setting is a dynamic process

It is important to keep in mind that goal setting is a journey, not a destination. Once you have begun the process, you should incorporate reflection as part of the goal setting process. To be effective, goal setting should be a continuous cycle. Remember to establish new goals as part of the process.

2 Goals must be well defined

Goals can help us to keep our focus and direction, even at times when things get complicated or confusing. They can help us make the right choices for ourselves. Goals are like magnets that pull you through life's difficult times. The more vivid and clear your goals, the more they help to keep you moving in the right direction.

3 Goals must be consistent with your values

If your goals do not match your values and beliefs, you will constantly be in conflict with yourself. This conflict can deplete your energy and motivation. Your goals should unify and balance your life, not divide it.

4 Be committed to your goals

All goals have a price. Reaching goals takes time and commitment. Depending on the goal, it may require personal or financial sacrifice. Success depends upon your ability to pay the price demanded.

5 Create an action plan

A goal without a plan is just a fantasy. Setting realistic goals is important; acting on them is even more important. It's not enough just to want to achieve something; you need to map out a plan, and put that plan into action.

6 Monitor your progress

Sometimes we get started toward a goal, only to discover that we do not have the means, skills, or abilities needed to achieve it. In such cases you must either change the goal or acquire the necessary means or skills. Remember, goal setting is a journey.

7 Make your goals realistic and challenging

Set goals that are achievable. Otherwise, you are creating an environment for failure. This isn't to say that you should avoid goals that appear to be difficult. Your desire to achieve a goal and your willingness to invest the necessary effort must be balanced with the difficulty of achieving it.

◄█8█ Keep your goals flexible

Today's world is in a constant state of flux. Jobs change, families change, and values change. Your life evolves over time, so it only makes sense to keep your goals flexible. Incorporate a change management system into your goals. That's not to say you should compromise your goals — only that you should recognize when it's time to change (or modify) a goal in order to reflect more realistically the direction you want to take.

◄█9█ Set goals to help you plan and control your life

Your goals are a way of planning and controlling your life. Remember, your life will unfold with or without your input. The choice is yours.

BRAINSTORMING

Setting goals requires that you consider all the possibilities. So you need to brainstorm — writing down any goal that occurs to you. Don't worry if a goal seems silly, trivial, or far-fetched. Write it down anyway. Later you can evaluate each goal and determine whether or not it's worth pursuing.

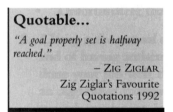

Quotable...

"A goal properly set is halfway reached."

– ZIG ZIGLAR
Zig Ziglar's Favourite
Quotations 1992

List goals in all areas of your life, not just your career. Be open to exploring new fields, opportunities, and interests. Think about the things you believe it takes to be successful, and set goals to develop yourself in those areas.

Goals guide you to your desired outcomes, so you shouldn't limit yourself in setting those goals. Ask yourself, *"If I did not have to worry about failure, what would I do?"*

Without inhibiting yourself, write down your goals for each area of your life: career, family, financial, hobbies, and personal health and fitness. Be concise, but be as descriptive as possible.

Goal Setting S.M.A.R.T.s

Are your goals S.M.A.R.T.? In other words, are they *Specific, Measurable, Achievable, Realistic,* and *Time-bound?* Let's consider each criterion in turn.

S PECIFIC Identify exactly what want to achieve. Goals such as *"I want a better job"* are too general to allow you to create a plan. Here it's worthwhile to look at a general goal, and break it down into specifics. For example, *"I want a better job"* might really mean *"I want to earn more money"* or *"I want a promotion"* or *"I want a similar job with a new company whose corporate values are more like my own."* Frame your goals in terms of a specific result. Then you can define a path to achieve them.

M EASURABLE Set out goals in such a way that you can measure your progress or achievement. To continue with the previous example, you won't know if you have a "better job" if you have not established the specific criteria which define it. On the other hand, you *can* measure a higher salary, a promotion, or a job more suited to your personal values.

A CHIEVABLE Unachievable goals can be worse than no goals at all. Why? Because you're almost bound to fail, and that will deplete your motivation. Better to set smaller, more achievable goals and update them frequently. Assess goals in the context of your abilities and available resources. List the resources you require to achieve the goal. Resources can be anything available to assist you, including people (specify *which* people and what role they'll play), courses, research facilities, financial resources, or information. It also helps to make sure your goals are consistent with your interests and capabilities.

R EALISTIC Goals that are realistic — that is, consistent with the other objectives in your life — are the most effective. Ask yourself if your goals are truly compatible with your personal vision. If goals in different areas of your life are not compatible, you will be pulled in different directions, and you will be undermining your ability to succeed.

T IME-BOUND Set a specific time frame for completing each of your goals. Setting time frames will motivate you to act, and to move continually towards your desired outcome. Goals without time frames are simply dreams which may or may not come true.

GOAL PLANS

How do we move from setting our goals to achieving them? Setting goals is an important part of clarifying our desired outcomes and our roles and responsibilities in life. But in order to be successful, we need a concrete strategy for achieving our goals. The way to begin the process of attaining our goals is to create a plan.

■ Define steps towards your goal

Lay your plans out so that each goal is broken down into the specific steps required to achieve it. These steps can include skill development, professional development, and research, among many others. Each step should contain only a single objective (one task, one course, etc.). This process allows us to construct our goals as a series of distinct, attainable "mini-goals" that are steadily moving us in the direction of our desired outcome.

■ Set completion dates

For each step towards the completion of your goals, it is wise to set a date when you must reach that step. A completion date should also be set for your final goal. Record all completion dates, as this allows you to measure your progress on an ongoing basis. Time allocation is also important to achieving your goals. Use the time management skills discussed in the next chapter to help you plan your time.

■ Be flexible, but firm

Finally, it is important to recognize that there may be occasions when we choose to change our plan. Our values change, and our personal vision changes over time. Continual review of our goal plans allows us to assess when a goal is no longer appropriate to our personal situation.

There are also times when circumstances are such that we need to modify, or compromise, our goal plans. Goal plans are flexible, and can change — although we should avoid modifying our goal plans just because we face difficulty. Indeed, the purpose of a goal plan is to help us continue towards our goal in the face of difficulties. Modify plans, if necessary, but be sure that you are continuing on your desired path, and that you are modifying plans for the right reasons. As long as changes are made for the right reasons — which do not include simply giving up — it does not mean failure.

LOSING CONVICTION

It's one of the most common reasons for failing to meet our objectives. We start off profoundly excited by a goal — starting a new business, perhaps, or using a new sales technique, or quitting smoking — and fully commit ourselves to it. Then we become distracted by some other matter; our mood changes, and we lose our conviction.

Self-discipline is an important part of accomplishing our goals. Ultimately, each of us is accountable for our own performance. One way that we can develop and manage our self-discipline is by creating a closed-loop process for achieving goals:

- Write your goals down.
- Place your written goals in a highly visible place, where you will see them throughout the day.
- Refer to your goal list and goal plan, often and consistently.
- Build your goal plan into a thorough time-management system. Allocate the time necessary to complete each step towards your goals. Write it down. Protect the time you schedule from other distractions or events. (See Chapter 9 for more details.)
- Communicate the priorities outlined in your goal plan to others.

Supercharged Goal Setting

Thinking about a goal on a weekly basis will yield a moderate level of success. Daily attention will enhance our chances substantially. But think about the effects of focusing on improvement every quarter-hour!

High performers ask themselves two questions on almost a minute-by-minute basis: *"Is what I am doing right now consistent with my goals?"* and *"What is my objective over the next 15-minute period?"*

One of the keys to this method of short-term, performance-oriented goal setting is to give yourself rewards and penalties. For example, *"If I return all my messages by 4 p.m. today, then I can have dessert after dinner tonight"* or *"If I'm not out of bed by 5 a.m., then I have to do an extra 15 minutes of house cleaning."*

- Assign a specific time and date for each step towards your goal in your time management system. Write it down.
- List completion dates for specific steps or tasks in your goal plan. Establish weekly and daily tasks.
- Act on each step you have written down. Identify your daily and weekly accomplishments.
- Plan rewards for accomplishing different steps in your goal plan.

BALANCE YOUR LIFE

One thing that many successful people share is balance in their lives. Their goals reflect their personal vision of their role, not just in one area of their lives, but in all areas.

When you assess your goal plan, ensure that it covers all the areas of life that are important to you. Do you have personal health goals? Goals for family life? Achieving a balance of goals is important to success.

To achieve this balance, clarify your roles and responsibilities in four key areas: family, career, community, and self. Then you can define your goals for each area and allocate your time accordingly. Also, be sure to allocate time to reflect and evaluate. Continual review of our goal plans allows us to ensure that our goals remain in balance with our personal vision.

SUMMARY

1. Success depends largely on being goal-oriented.

2. There are many reasons why people don't set goals. Being aware of them will help you to avoid the same pitfalls.

3. There are nine principles of effective goal setting.

4. The effectiveness of goals can be evaluated with the S.M.A.R.T. (*Specific, Measurable, Achievable, Realistic,* and *Time-bound*) test.

5. Developing specific plans to achieve your goals is essential if you want to avoid losing your conviction.

6. Goals should reflect a healthy balance of business and personal needs.

Time Management

One of the biggest challenges facing salespeople today is the management of many responsibilities in a limited amount of time. We can meet this challenge through the effective application of time-management skills.

HOW DO YOU MANAGE?

Every time we make a choice about what to do at work we are making a time-management decision. Making that decision effectively depends on whether we manage our time, or whether we let our time manage us.

Below are two lists, each documenting a specific type of behaviour. One is that of a good organizer and time manager; the other is that of an individual with poor time-management skills. Which sounds more like you?

GOOD TIME MANAGER	BAD TIME MANAGER
• generally seems calm	• often appears stressed or tense
• remains calm in a crisis	• cannot seem to deal with a crisis
• is always organized	• often seems disorganized
• is good at his/her job, fulfills all responsibilities, and usually achieves goals	• has trouble fulfilling the responsibilities of his/her job
• has no trouble setting priorities and delegating (does not try to do it all him/herself)	• has trouble setting priorities and delegating (tries to do it all)
• leads a balanced life	• feels a conflict between work and private life, appears to regret spending too much time at one or the other

Time-management skills are directly linked to personal self-talk. No one is born a poor time manager; rather, it is a matter of personal habits.

For example, a salesperson who is not productive in the morning may not be getting enough sleep; he or she may also have developed a cluster of negative self-talk that interferes with morning productivity. Similarly, if you are not productive in the afternoon, the reason could be a poor diet or a cluster of negative self-talk that kicks in after lunch.

Conflict assessment

How much conflict is there between your work life and your personal life? The following questionnaire will help to determine this.

	STRONGLY DISAGREE (1)	MILDLY DISAGREE (2)	MILDLY AGREE (3)	STRONGLY AGREE (4)
My job interferes too much with my personal life				
I resent the need to work overtime/nights/weekends.				
I cannot seem to leave my problems at work.				
I do not feel in control of my life as much as I would like.				
I feel guilty for not spending enough time with my family, friends, church. etc.				
I find that bringing home work is frustrating.				
If i were better organized, I could spend more time doing things that give me the most satisfaction.				
I sometimes have personal problems that affect my concentration at work.				
Some family or close friends feel I give too much to the job and not enough to them.				
My personal responsibilities sometimes sap the energy I need to do my job effectively.				

HOW DID YOU SCORE?

* *If you strongly agreed with any one of the 10 statements* in the questionnaire, you have a conflict that requires attention.

* *If you agreed (strongly or mildly) with more statements than you disagreed with (strongly or mildly)*, there is a significant conflict between your work and personal life.

* *If you strongly agreed to 5 or more of the statements*, there is probably a conflict between your work and personal life that is seriously affecting your performance, your personal relationships, or both.

UNDERSTANDING CONFLICTS

The questionnaire is designed to point out conflicts that may exist between your work life and personal life. It examines your attitudes. Each attitude stated in the question is a negative attitude. Your strong agreement with any one, or your predominant agreement with all of them, indicates a negative attitude towards the relationship between your personal and professional life. Conflicts occur when people do not accept the reality of the workplace or do not view their work as a priority. These conflicts are the result of attitude.

Attitude can be managed, as can the conflicts identified in the questionnaire. Each can be traced to a conflict in use of time — for example, problems at home invading time at work, or having more work than can be completed within reasonable hours of the day. The first step in managing these conflicts is to understand the specific causes of the conflicts between your work and personal life.

■ Time-management assessment

On the next few pages, you will find a four-part questionnaire that is designed to help you identify specific time-management problems so that you can start resolving them.

Try to answer all questions in all four sections as honestly as you can. This is essential if you are to find answers to your time-management problems.

As in the previous questionnaire, simply indicate with a check mark whether you strongly agree, mildly agree, mildly disagree, or strongly disagree with the statement as it applies to you.

Time-Management Assessment (Part 1)

Organizing Yourself	Strongly Disagree (1)	Mildly Disagree (2)	Mildly Agree (3)	Strongly Agree (4)
I often take work home.				
I tend to underestimate the time it will take to do something.				
Because I am a bit of a perfectionist, I get too bogged down in detail.				
My work area is usually cluttered and disorganized.				
I do not have clearly-defined career or personal goals.				
I am not a morning person. It takes me some time to get operational.				
I tend to put off unpleasant work.				
Approaching a deadline makes me work a lot harder				
I often find myself shuffling paper, accomplishing little.				
I tend to do easy or fun things first.				
I have trouble getting started on some tasks or projects.				
I do not work effectively when I have a lot of different things to do.				
I work more overtime hours than I think is reasonable.				
I can never catch up on the reading I need to do.				
I spend too little time devising better or faster ways of doing things.				

INTERPRETING YOUR SCORE (PAGES 96 AND 97)

- Any statement with which you agree strongly indicates a specific problem you need to work on.
- If you strongly agree with four or more statements or agree strongly or mildly with more than eight statements, you have a serious problem that is having a negative impact on your performance and job satisfaction. Make a note of these time-management strengths and weaknesses.

Time-Management Assessment (Part 2)

ORGANIZING YOUR JOB	STRONGLY DISAGREE (1)	MILDLY DISAGREE (2)	MILDLY AGREE (3)	STRONGLY AGREE (4)
I do not have clear written job objectives that define the results I am expected to achieve.				
I do not really know or understand the criteria on which my performance is measured.				
Many of my tasks or projects don't have expected completion dates.				
I am involved in a lot of crisis management and fire-fighting.				
I do not have a clearly-defined development plan for myself.				
I do not keep a list of things to do.				
I rarely take time to reviewcrtically my progress towards my objectives.				
Constantly changing priorities make it difficult to plan my work.				
I spend less than 10% of my time planning.				
I have no specific process for establishing priorities.				
Some of my important responsibilities do not get the time and attention they deserve.				
Much of my time is spent reacting to the needs and demands of others.				
I do not have a clear picture of my boss's objectives and priorities.				
I tend not to schedule my work. I only schedule meetings and appointments.				
I miss deadlines too often.				

Time-Management Assessment (Part 3)

ORGANIZING YOUR RELATIONSHIPS	STRONGLY DISAGREE (1)	MILDLY DISAGREE (2)	MILDLY AGREE (3)	STRONGLY AGREE (4)
Interruptions make it difficult for me to work efficiently.				
I am always accessible to those who need my help or advice.				
I find it difficult to say no to people who want my help.				
I probably spend too much time socializing with my co-workers.				
Some people seem to take up an inordinate amount of my time.				
Not much of the time I spend with my boss is on a regular, scheduled basis.				
I spend too much time in meetings.				
Most meetings I attend are too long and inefficient.				
I rarely worry about interrupting or wasting the time of others.				
I believe in an open door policy.				
Others I work with do not understand my objectives or priorities.				
I spend too much time involved in interdepartmental or interpersonal conflicts.				
I do not spend enough uninterrupted time with my boss.				
I do not spend enough uninterrupted time with co-workers/customers/etc.				

INTERPRETING YOUR SCORE (PAGES 98 AND 99)

- Any statement with which you agree strongly indicates a specific problem you need to work on.
- If you strongly agree with four or more statements or agree strongly or mildly with more than eight statements, you have a serious problem that is having a negative impact on your performance and job satisfaction. Make a note of these time-management strengths and weaknesses.

Time-Management Assessment (Part 4)

ORGANIZING YOUR SYSTEMS	STRONGLY DISAGREE (1)	MILDLY DISAGREE (2)	MILDLY AGREE (3)	STRONGLY AGREE (4)
My job requires me to do too much paperwork.				
I hate writing reports.				
Many reports around here are never read or acted upon.				
I have to spend too much time getting the information I need.				
I have not used a time log in the past year.				
My telephone is a constant source of interruptions.				
A lot of time is wasted on *telephone tag*.				
Our telecommunications system is not efficient.				
Our communications systems (mail, E-mail, secretarial, etc.) need Improvement.				
Many of our policies, rules, and procedures are bureaucratic.				
I do not have a good follow-up system.				
My personal files are not well organized.				
I spend a lot of time getting information for other people.				
I do not know enough about how our systems work.				
I wish someone would help me organize how to do some things.				

TIME-MANAGEMENT OBSTACLES

Even the most well organized salespeople encounter obstacles that interfere with their work. It takes considerable effort to avoid or eliminate these obstacles. Here we'll examine five of the most common obstacles and how you can overcome them.

◀1 Personal interruptions

Because we generally do not work in isolated environments, our work is often interrupted by our peers. The following are some suggestions to help you handle personal interruptions. Consider the nature of your own personal interruptions and devise strategies to eliminate or limit them.

- Go to the other person's office or meet that person halfway.
- Announce a time limit at the beginning of the conversation. For example, *"I can give you 15 minutes."*
- Get to the point assertively: *"How can I help you?"*
- Consider scheduling regular staff meetings if you are frequently interrupted.
- Stand up when someone enters your office. If he or she stays too long, slowly start to walk out of your office and down the hall. The person will follow. Then excuse yourself and get back to work.

◀2 Telephone interruptions

Consider the kinds of telephone interruptions you experience and create a plan to minimize them. Keep in mind, however, that incoming telephone calls (for salespeople) can also be quite valuable — particularly if it means new business. Therefore, you need to maintain a careful balance. Here are some suggestions to help you handle telephone interruptions.

- Schedule blocks of time for making phone calls.
- Get to the point quickly.
- Use a call screener.
- Ask yourself, *"Do I really need to talk to this person?"*
- Use time-saving technologies, such as cellular phones, electronic mail, fax machines, and voice-mail.

In Practice

Re-examine the specific problem areas you identified in the question-naire on pages 96-99. On a sheet of paper — and keeping in mind the solutions we have suggested to various time-management obstacles — list the areas that need attention. For each problem area, consider a plan for improvement.

For example, let's say that you identify one of your problems as *"Most meetings I attend are too long and inefficient"* (time-management questionnaire, part 3; page 98). Your plan might be: *"For our next meeting I will prepare an agenda with a specific time frame for each item to be discussed."*

Each problem, with its potential solution(s), should also be assessed in terms of its urgency and importance. This will help to ensure you are developing a plan that is consistent with your personal vision, roles, and responsibilities.

3 Meetings

While meetings provide an important forum for sharing information and ideas, they can also be great time wasters. Effective management will ensure that the time spent in a meeting has value. Here are some suggestions to help you manage your meeting time better.

- Prepare and distribute an agenda.
- Assign specific time frames to each item on the agenda.
- For each meeting, appoint someone to keep the meeting on track.
- Start meetings on time; don't wait for latecomers.
- Hold brief, stand-up meetings. People will become restless after about 10 minutes, so meetings won't drag on too long.

4 Desk organization

A poorly organized desk can have a negative effect on your job performance. Unless you are organized, you can't find important information when you need it, you spend too much time looking for materials, and you become distracted by work that is not your top priority. Here are some suggestions for keeping a well-organized desk.

- Design your work area so that regularly used items are within reach.

- Computerize your work as much as possible.
- Reduce paperwork by communicating face to face or by phone — it's faster and easier, too.
- Clean your desk every week.
- Throw out what you don't need.
- Act on all incoming paperwork immediately.
- Try to handle each piece of incoming mail only once.
- Do not respond to mail in writing if a phone call or fax can do the job.

Procrastination

Most of us procrastinate to some degree; the important thing is to resist the temptation to put things off. Otherwise, the result can be missed deadlines, added stress in meeting deadlines, and wasted time at work. Try some of the following suggestions to help minimize procrastination.

- Live 15 minutes at a time.
- Start something you've been postponing.
- Designate a specific time for a task you've been putting off.
- Look hard at your life. Are you doing what you would choose to do if you had six months to live?
- Decide not to be tired until the moment before you get into bed.
- Eliminate the words "hope," "wish," "should," and "maybe" from your vocabulary.
- Ask yourself, *"What is the best use of my time right now?"*
- When you make a commitment to do something, write it down or tell it to someone.
- Take exclusive, personal responsibility for your projects.
- Work in small steps.

PLANNING FOR SUCCESS

While there's much to be said for getting the job done sooner rather than later, it's important to remember the role of planning in effective time management.

We all know the saying, "Don't just sit there — do something!" Well, planning can be summed up in the complementary phrase, "Don't just do something — sit there!"

In other words, you needn't be addressing an item from your to-do list at every moment during the day; sometimes it's more effective to spend some time planning. With planning, you work smarter — and therefore faster. In fact, studies suggest that one minute of planning can save up to eight minutes of work time.

The remainder of this chapter will examine some concepts and tools that will help you in your efforts to plan your time more effectively.

Urgency and importance

The first step in effective planning is to assign priorities for the various tasks you have to complete. You can categorize these tasks in two ways — according to *urgency* and *importance*.

Urgency describes the relative immediacy of a required activity. Urgent tasks demand a reaction. They are usually visible and easier to attend to than other tasks. For example, a ringing phone is urgent.

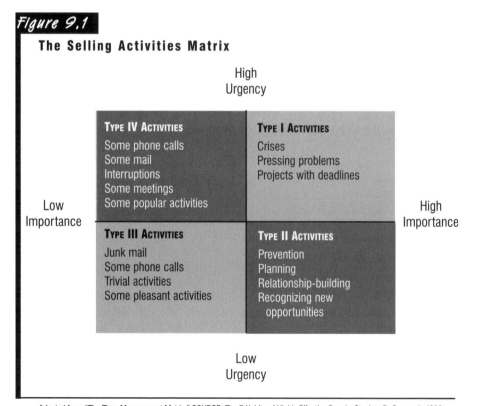

Figure 9.1

The Selling Activities Matrix

High Urgency

TYPE IV ACTIVITIES	TYPE I ACTIVITIES
Some phone calls Some mail Interruptions Some meetings Some popular activities	Crises Pressing problems Projects with deadlines
TYPE III ACTIVITIES	**TYPE II ACTIVITIES**
Junk mail Some phone calls Trivial activities Some pleasant activities	Prevention Planning Relationship-building Recognizing new opportunities

Low Importance · High Importance

Low Urgency

Adapted from "The Time Management Matrix." SOURCE: *The 7 Habits of Highly Effective People*, Stephen R. Covey, © 1989.

Importance describes the relative value of an activity. If an activity contributes to your goals and values, it is probably important. Such tasks usually require timely action, although they may be more difficult to attend to than other matters.

You can classify your daily activities according to each of these criteria and assign them to one of four quadrants in a matrix. As shown in Figure 9.1 (previous page), each quadrant represents one of four general types of activities, where the horizontal axis indicates relative importance and the vertical axis indicates relative urgency.

Salespeople often underestimate the volume of things they must accomplish during the day; therefore, they often feel pressured or constrained when unanticipated tasks arise. Most people tend to assess priority in terms of urgency, but do not take into consideration the importance of a task. Both urgency and importance are significant for making better decisions.

Ideally, you should spend as much of your time as possible dealing with Type II activities. In order to do this, you need to develop a process for choosing work activities.

☑ *Personal Check*

Time-management techniques

☐ Plan your travel routes for efficiency and effectiveness.

☐ Use your waiting time effectively — read, answer mail, write memos, plan your next week, etc.

☐ Take advantage of technology — voice-mail, fax, contact management systems, etc.

☐ Delegate where possible. Make use of support people, colleagues, customers, supervisors, etc.

☐ Assess all your resources — people, technology, support systems.

☐ Be open to change and constantly look for ways to improve effectiveness, efficiency, and productivity.

☐ Assess the ways in which you spend your time. Establish your personal best practices.

SET PRIORITIES

Here the key is to identify which activities are important and which are not. This should help virtually eliminate all Type III and Type IV activities, because whether a matter is urgent or not, if it is not important, you should try to avoid spending time on it.

DELEGATE URGENT TASKS

Where appropriate, some high-urgency/high-importance tasks (Type 1 activities) can be passed on to employees, colleagues, or even your boss. The important thing is to avoid trying to do everything yourself. If you delegate matters to other people you will make more of your time available for Type II activities.

In Practice

What's Your Time Worth?

The expression "time is money" is so familiar that we often do not stop to consider its basic truth. As a salesperson, every hour that you spend working represents an expense to your employer. Your value, then, is measured by the sales you generate relative to that cost.

For any given period, most salespeople know their sales volume. But what's the cost of your time? This is expressed by the formula

$$\text{Cost per hour} = \frac{\text{Direct cost of employee}}{\text{Working hours}}$$

Your direct costs include salary, bonuses, commissions, travel expenses, and miscellaneous contributions (to UIC and pensions, for example) and other expenses. In a typical year, you'll work about 1,880 hours.

Consider the following example. Try calculating your cost per hour.

	Jo Smith	You
Salary	$30,000	
Commissions	12,000	
Travel	10,000	
Direct cost	$54,000	
Working hours	1,880	1,880
Cost per hour	$28.72	

Once you've determined your cost per hour, consider the activities you undertake in light of their cost. Your working day consists of many activities — prospecting, administration, marketing, selling, and reporting. It's important to understand that time spent on non-revenue-generating activities has a cost that must be recouped during your selling hours.

Plan your many activities with the value of your time in mind. Determine the priority of your activities, then assign a percentage of your working hours to each. (We'll be looking at this concept more closely in Part 4: Strategic Selling Skills.)

By employing these strategies you'll be able to eliminate Type III and Type IV activities, while minimizing Type I activities, leaving you more time to take a planning-oriented approach to your work.

Evaluating the relative urgency and importance of tasks — and establishing priorities for them — is yet another instance of where you can demonstrate the behaviour of an agent, not a victim.

USING A PERSONAL ORGANIZER

All salespeople need to keep a personal organizer — whether in the form of a traditional *diary, appointment book, planner,* or, more recently, an *electronic organizer* or *personal digital assistant (PDA)*. Unfortunately, while many people have personal planners, they don't use them — at least, not effectively.

Here are a few suggestions for getting the most out of your personal organizer.

* Make, manage, and maintain a to-do list for each day.
* Delegate and establish priorities for the items on the list based on the urgency/importance matrix discussed earlier. Move less important items to other days, remove them, or leave them on the list for today. Ideally, your to-do list should focus on Type II activities.
* Rely on your organizer. Carry it everywhere you go — even to

Good Times, Bad Times

Everyone has a preferred time for getting work done — usually a block of three or four hours when you are typically most productive, creative, and focused. Conversely, there are times in the day when you tend to be more lethargic, unfocused, and distracted.

Try to become more aware of these good and bad times, and schedule your time accordingly. Block off time for the more important tasks (those requiring your best, creative, focused efforts) during your good times.

Don't be a slave to these times, however. Good times and bad times are not biologically determined; rather, they are based on an individual's psychology and self-talk. Teach yourself to recognize why good times and bad times occur. Use positive self-talk and attitude maintenance techniques to break any negative patterns.

lunch. Be sure that it contains an alphabetized listing of all the phone numbers and addresses you may need some day. Don't leave little pieces of paper with people's phone numbers lying around. Record in your book when you need to call someone and include that person's phone number.

- Block off time in your daily schedule for each item on the list. Account for interruptions and delays in your scheduling by allowing for extra time. Consider your tasks, projects, and responsibilities as if they were people. The time you block off for these tasks should be treated like an appointment with a person. Commit to the time and don't miss the appointment.

- Throughout the day, review your schedule and to-do list. Reschedule and establish priorities as required. Carry over to tomorrow what you did not get done today.

- Schedule personal development time, and time for goal-setting. Your success depends upon your continued movement towards your desired outcomes. Try to keep this in mind when planning your daily and weekly activities.

- Don't forget to block off time for planning. Use this time to plan at least one week ahead. Update schedules and to-do lists, and block off appointments as required.

- Use your organizer while you sort through the paper on your desk. On trays, or at the side of your desk, pile all pieces of paper or files, one at a time, in two different piles: "sooner" and "later." Go over each piece of paper before you place it in a pile and decide what has to be done to that piece of paper. In your book, record what has to be done — and when. Break down your larger tasks into smaller steps. This way, you won't have to worry about forgetting something, since it will all be recorded in one place. Just follow the list of what has to be done on a given day. At the end of every day, completely straighten up your work area.

- Resolve to rely on your organizer at all times. Don't allow yourself to waver.

In Chapter 8 we discussed the concept of a *closed-loop system* — a series of checks and balances to help you keep track of your activities and responsibilities. It helps you prevent things from being forgotten or missed. When used properly, your appointment book or organizer serves as a closed-loop system.

COPING WITH CHANGES

In a perfect world, time management would simply be a matter of creating a schedule and sticking with it. But the fact is we must deal with unexpected changes to our schedule. Many people have a natural tendency to resist dealing with unexpected changes. But this is the behaviour of a victim — and, as we've stressed throughout this book, we want to be agents.

To deal effectively with changes to an established schedule, think of every project or task in terms of three, interdependent variables, called the "triple-threat constraints": *cost, performance* (or *quality*), and *timing*. These variables are interdependent, so changes to one affect the other two. It helps to think of the variables as the sides of a triangle. If one side changes, the others must accommodate it to maintain the structure's integrity.

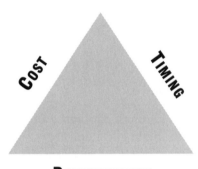

PERFORMANCE

For example, let's say that you are preparing a report for a customer and he or she wants to add more details — in other words, increase the *performance* or *quality* variable in the project. Here, you should (tactfully) let the customer know that incorporating the change is not a problem. It means, however, that the *timing* and/or *cost* of the project will also be modified. Explain how these variables are interdependent. The customer must therefore decide which is most important — report modifications (*performance*), timing, or cost.

MANAGING MULTIPLE PROJECTS

In today's business environment, salespeople are often called upon to manage several projects and responsibilities at once. Some people use a formalized system to manage their multiple projects and deadlines. Many people do not; as a result, they run into problems.

Think for a moment about the system you use to manage your workload. Does your system ever fail you? Be honest — do you always finish projects on time? Is everything you do finished to perfection? Do you feel you have the right amount of work to do and enough time to do it? Are you always relaxed and in control? For many people, the answer to these questions is "No."

Tips for Managing Multiple Projects

Here are a few suggestions to assist you in managing multiple projects successfully. These tips assume you have an effective time-management system, as outlined in previous sections.

- Set a clear project goal and sub-goals.

- Outline a detailed, time-bound critical path of all the steps involved in a project.

- Break down large projects into smaller action steps and tasks.

- Assign individuals to be responsible for each task.

- Define accurate specifications and deadlines.

- Hold debriefing sessions.

- Colour-code projects.

- Work on only one thing at a time and move everything else off your desk.

- Make time to get that lagging project back on track.

- Organize your desk at the end of the day.

- Put each project on a separate clipboard.

- Plan one week in advance. Create daily and weekly action plans. Record them in your date book and stick to them.

- Negotiate a specific budget for each project.

- Schedule time for all the tasks involved in every project. Be sure to set aside enough time for complex or time-consuming tasks.

- Keep a journal for each project.

SUMMARY

1. There is a clear relationship between effective time management and sales success.

2. In order to excel, salespeople are called upon to do more than seems humanly possible: to become effective at managing multiple projects, responsibilities, and deadlines, and to capitalize on every available opportunity. These things require superior time–management skills.

3. Effective time management begins with an understanding of your personal strengths and weaknesses in this area. You have been able to gain this understanding with the questionnaires presented in this chapter.

4. A *closed-loop system* allows you to meet the time-management challenges you face on a daily basis. By using this system and the concepts discussed in this chapter you will prevent things from falling through the cracks, thus improving your ability to manage the limited time you have available. This improvement will serve you well in your efforts to maximize the return you generate in your sales territory, as well as help you achieve personal success.

Stress Management

Stress is a double-edged sword. All of us (even animals) rely on stress in order to survive. On the other hand, excessive or unmanaged stress can be extremely unhealthy (if not deadly). Therefore, it's wise for us to learn to recognize and manage our own stress.

TYPES OF STRESS

There is good stress and there is bad stress. Hunger is one example of good stress. The stress of hunger causes us to eat when our body requires food. A job promotion may cause stress because of the change it causes in our lives, but for most people it is usually good news. It is stress that causes us to laugh, and this release has a beneficial effect.

Arguing causes bad stress. Having to complete multiple tasks in too little time can cause bad stress. Bad stress results from not dealing effectively with a situation.

No matter what type of stress we experience, however, we can benefit from learning to deal with it effectively in order to improve efficiency and sales performance.

■ Measuring your stress index

Excessive or unmanaged stress can have severe physical, psychological, and emotional effects. Yet we often don't realize when stress becomes unhealthy. The habits, attitudes, and signs that can alert us to problems may be unrecognized because they have become familiar.

A stress index is a measuring tool designed to help determine if your stress levels are unhealthy. Answer the questions below to find out. Answer each question as honestly as possible; take your time and complete each question. If you have any hesitation over a question, then the answer is usually "Yes."

Do you frequently...	YES	NO
Neglect your diet?		
Try to do everything?		
Blow up easily?		
Seek unrealistic goals?		
Fail to see the humour in situations others find funny?		
Act rudely?		
Make a "big deal" of everything?		
Look to other people to make things happen?		
Have difficulty making decisions?		
Complain you are disorganized?		
Avoid people whose ideas are different from your own?		
Keep everything inside?		
Neglect exercise?		
Lack supportive relationships?		
Use psychoactive drugs, like sleeping pills and tranquilizers, without a physician's approval?		
Get too little rest?		
Get angry when you are kept waiting?		
Ignore stress symptoms?		
Procrastinate?		
Think there is only one right way to do something?		
Fail to build in relaxation time?		
Gossip?		
Race through the day?		
Spend a lot of time feeling badly about the past?		
Fail to get a break from noise and crowds?		

Index adapted from *60 Ways To Make Stress Work For You*, by Andrew F. Slavy, M.D., Ph.D. P.P.H; PIA Press, 1988

STRESS INDEX SCORING

Score 1 for each "yes" answer, and 0 for each "no" answer. Your total score can be interpreted as follows:

Under 7   There are few hassles in your life. Make sure, though, that you are not trying so hard to avoid problems that you shy away from challenges.

7 to 13   You've got your life in pretty good control. Work on the choices and habits that could still be causing some unnecessary stress in your life.

14 to 20   You're approaching the danger zone. You may well be suffering stress-related symptoms and your relationships could be strained. Think carefully about choices you've made and take relaxation breaks every day.

Over 20   Emergency! You must stop now, rethink how you are living, change your attitudes, and pay scrupulous attention to your diet, exercise, and relaxation programs.

MANAGING STRESS

Perhaps the most important critical factor in managing your stress is to recognize that a salesperson's job is naturally stressful. Understanding that stress is always going to be a part of your working life, you can then develop attitudes and strategies to deal with it in a more positive way.

Teach yourself not to take things personally. You are in a professional environment. Remember to view things as a professional. Develop an optimistic attitude and view problems as temporary and local. Take an agent-oriented approach to solving them. Use positive self-talk to turn negative and stressful situations around.

Part of dealing with stress in the workplace is to know when you need to let something go, even temporarily. Take a break if you absolutely need it in order to re-focus yourself and approach the situation in a more positive way. Make sure that you have other things in your life to focus on when you are away from work. This will prevent you from taking your stress home with you.

Keep yourself healthy, and exercise regularly. Exercise is a critical factor in relieving and managing stress.

Tips for Low-Stress Working

Outlined below are some general tips for dealing with the stress you face in your job as a sales professional.

- **Build rewarding, cooperative relationships** with as many of your colleagues and employees as possible.

- **Rank your work by importance** and manage your time effectively; don't take on more than you can handle.

- **Take the initiative** in as many problem areas as you can; get a jump on them before they build up.

- **Build an effective and supportive relationship** with your boss. Understand his or her problems and help your boss to understand yours. Ensure that your boss understands your workload, and work together to keep assignments reasonable.

- **Negotiate realistic deadlines** on important projects with your boss. Be prepared to propose deadlines yourself, rather than have them imposed.

- **Learn as much as you can about upcoming events**. Anticipate wherever possible. Be proactive, not reactive.

- **Find time every day for detachment and relaxation.** Use your breaks to put your feet up, relax deeply, and take your mind off work. Use pleasant thoughts or images to refresh your mind.

- **Get away from your workstation** from time to time for a change of scene and a change of mind. Don't eat lunch at your desk or linger long after work is finished.

- **Reduce the amount of time spent on trivial tasks** that are not your responsibility.

- **Delegate when appropriate**. However, don't get this confused with avoiding unpleasant tasks that are part of your responsibility.

- **Don't put off dealing with distasteful tasks or problems**. Accept short-term stress instead of long-term anxiety and discomfort.

- **Make a constructive "problem list."** Write down the problems that concern you and what you plan to do about them. Get them out into the open where you can deal with them.

SUMMARY

1. Stress is unavoidable — especially for a salesperson.

2. Stress is necessary to survive. If left uncontrolled, however, stress can have a negative impact on your health, performance, personal relationships, and success.

3. There a number of key factors that determine your stress level. These are identified in the questionnaire on page 112.

4. You can employ stress-management strategies, such as those featured on the previous page, to improve productivity, increase happiness, and enhance personal success.

Business Knowledge

One key area of self-management involves ensuring that you have up-to-date and extensive knowledge about the products you sell and the environment and market in which you operate. As with the other factors which influence our success, business knowledge can be developed and managed.

In this chapter we will be examining some of the general principles involved in developing business knowledge — recognizing, of course, that the specifics will very much depend on the type of products you sell. (Please note that wherever we refer to "products," this can mean products and/or services.)

PRODUCT KNOWLEDGE

As a sales professional, customers expect you to be knowledgeable about what you sell. Through this knowledge you are able to establish faith in your product and trust in you as a salesperson.

Product knowledge is critical to many aspects of your job as a sales professional. Your interactions with customers — that is, where you employ tactical selling skills — are affected by your product knowledge, as is your sales planning (strategic selling skills).

Developing technical knowledge

Technical knowledge is the information base you use in order to sell your products or services. With it, you can respond to basic questions with up-to-date, complete, and accurate answers. This information can be committed to memory or documented and kept with you at all times.

Typically, technical knowledge will include:

- product pricing;

- lead times;
- how products are manufactured or sourced;
- components of the product;
- warranty or guarantee policies;
- product evolution and history;
- packaging facilities and potential; and
- any awards that distinguish the product.

Be sure your information is current, so customers don't have to wait for you to get back to them with answers to their questions. Spending time in the field with technical specialists will give depth and timeliness to your technical understanding of your products.

Keep abreast of all product promotions, sales manuals, and product literature. Try to make reading this material one of your professional development goals.

Identifying Value-Added Features

Today, customers expect value-added to be more than just an occasional offering. So adding value should be an essential feature of your sales plan. Successful salespeople ask themselves *"How can I add value?"* as part of their standard practice.

Providing value-added features and service simply means exceeding your customer's expectations. Look at each step in the process of your relationship with your customers. Consider their specific needs and ask yourself, *"Is there some way I can step out of my routine and offer something more, better, or faster?"*

The important thing here is to understand what your customer is buying — not what you are selling. What you're selling is a solution to a problem or a benefit to the customer's operation. Once you understand what a customer really wants to buy (that is, a solution or benefit), you will find opportunities for adding value with your product.

When determining value-added features, keep in mind the profit margin on your product. After all, you don't want to add value to your customers without retaining value for your company.

Finally, remember that adding value is not a one-time process. Your competitors will catch up unless you add value on a continuous basis.

◼ Creating a product analysis

In order to sell effectively, it's important to know more than the basic facts about your products. You also need to examine and analyze your products' strengths, features, benefits, and weaknesses. This information should be incorporated into your sales plan.

The following is a list of key things you should know about your product. You may have to do some research to answer all the questions. Discussing these issues with your peers will also help you to clarify your understanding of your product, and how it is seen in the market.

- What are the essential selling features?
- What are the strengths and weaknesses of your product?
- What is the profit margin on your product?
- Does your product enjoy brand loyalty? What is the nature, or basis, of that loyalty?
- What is the market position of your product relative to that of your competitors?
- Who is using your product?

KNOW YOUR COMPETITION

Any analysis of your own product should also include an analysis of your competitors' market offerings. Knowing what the competition has to offer can make your job easier. Keep abreast of your competitors through their product promotions, brochures, and other sales materials.

Develop your understanding of their products and services as diligently as you develop your understanding of your own. Ask yourself: *"What are the selling features of the competition?"*; *"What are the advantages of my product over the competition?"*; and *"What are the disadvantages?"*

If you understand the answers to these questions clearly, you can develop a sales plan that capitalizes on both your product strengths and weaknesses. For example, if your competitor's products are less expensive, you can develop a sales plan that focuses on your product's superior quality or resilience.

Compare the success of each of your products relative to its direct competitors. Analyze your findings to determine the key benefits of your competitors' products. How do you account for your competitors' successes, and how can you address these issues in your sales plans? (These issues are examined further in Chapter 13: Territory Planning.)

MAKING THE LINK TO YOUR CUSTOMER
Your products have a number of features, applications, strengths, and weaknesses. In developing your technical and product knowledge, make sure you consider issues from the customer's perspective. How will your customer use the product? How can the product benefit your customer?

Translate each feature of your product into a benefit for the customer. Understand how your product fits into your customer's overall operation. Does your offering help to increase sales or lower costs? These issues may differ between customers, so examine product benefits as they relate to individual accounts. For example, same-day delivery may be a key feature which, for some accounts, may translate into improved operations, the ability to extend deadlines, or simple convenience. For other accounts, however, it may offer no real benefit.

✔ *Personal Check*

Do you know your product?

☐ Are you prepared to answer all questions about your product?

☐ Can you frame the features of your product to address a specific customer need, tailoring them to individual applications?

☐ Are you prepared for questions about your product's weaknesses or comparisons between your product and the competition's?

☐ Can you state your value-added features?

☐ Can you identify your product successes?

ADMINISTRATIVE, REGULATORY AND LEGAL KNOWLEDGE

Professional salespeople operate within a framework of policies, standards, regulations, and legal obligations. To conduct yourself properly in this context, you need to learn about the rules governing your industry.

▬ Understanding government legislation

Corporately and individually, we have a legal obligation to understand and comply with all government legislation concerning our industry. You are obliged to follow all federal, provincial, and local regulations. This means familiarizing yourself with the specific regulations that govern you. Some legislation will be specific to your province, region, and industry. However, everyone is affected by federal legislation, such as

- The Sale of Goods Act;
- The Consumer Protection Act; and
- The Competition Act.

You should also investigate any other federal and provincial statutes that apply to you, as well as any impending legislation that may affect your industry. In addition, keep track of recent legal settlements and rulings that affect you and the way you do business.

LICENCING AND GOVERNING BODIES

Make sure you obtain all necessary licences and certifications required to operate in your area. In communicating with governing bodies, respond promptly and appropriately. By understanding your obligations to governing bodies and fulfilling them expediently, you behave as an agent, not a victim.

Finally, in creating a workplace that protects and respects the individual, make sure that you follow all current employment standards. These standards include legislation governing human rights, equity, and harassment.

Understanding and using contracts

Contracts can be a significant component of the selling process. Negotiating and re-negotiating contracts with your customers and suppliers helps to provide a solid understanding of each party's obligations and compensations. Understanding contract law can be a valuable asset in your job as a salesperson. Pay particular attention to contract law as it pertains to your product, service, company, and industry.

When preparing contracts be sure to define the elements required. Anticipate contingencies — cost overruns, for example, or failure of the customer to meet their obligations — and what remedies or actions are available to each party in the contract. This will prevent misunderstandings or problems later in the relationship.

The nature of your company and your customer's company can affect your contract, so be sure to identify and understand the different forms of corporations and companies. These include: *sole proprietorships*; *partnerships*; *limited companies*; *corporations*; *not-for-profit organizations*; *cooperatives*; and *franchises*. Make sure you know the implications of events such as bankruptcy, changes of ownership, and other issues that can affect your contract.

Most importantly, honour your contracts. Whether they are written or verbal, a contract is an important legal and professional obligation.

EMPLOYMENT CONTRACTS

An employment contract is essential to safeguard both the company's interests and the interests of its employees. It defines an employee's legal responsibilities to the company, typically including those pertaining to conflicts of interest, non-disclosure, and trade secrets. For employees, it defines employer obligations such as salary, expenses, hours of work, benefits, and bonuses. For both parties it provides a solid understanding of obligations and compensations.

Assessing liability and insurance needs

Depending on the nature of your business, you may need to consider the issue of potential liability. Find out what circumstances, if any, can result in personal or professional liability, and protect yourself accordingly. (This is another instance of agent behaviour — preparing for liability instead of waiting until it's too late.) Be sure to carry the proper insurance coverage, whenever appropriate.

Complying with corporate policies

As a professional, you should follow all corporate policies and standards. These vary from organization to organization, and you should familiarize yourself with any policy manuals and literature available from your employer. Typical areas of corporate policy include

- Use of company patents, trademarks and copyrights.
- Corporate identification standards, such as the use of the company logo in communications.
- Protection of corporate intellectual property.

Adhering to industry standards

For each industry, there may be comprehensive standards to follow. As well, there are international standards that span industries. For example, ISO 9000 is an international standard dedicated to quality assurance. Ability to meet these types of standards tells your customers that you can provide high-quality products that are appropriate to their needs.

Familiarize yourself with industry standards for products, customer service, and all other aspects of your work and industry. Follow the trends in industry standards, and consider how your company or products measure up to those standards.

Undertake to meet (or exceed) industry standards, and measure your progress towards (or beyond) those standards. Find out how your competitors rate against industry standards and what they are doing to meet and exceed those standards. For information on administrative, regulatory, and legal issues, contact your local government office or library.

FINANCIAL KNOWLEDGE

What about the bottom line? Here's where it is important to have the necessary financial knowledge. This comprises not only your financial status, needs and obligations, but also those of your company and your customer.

▬ Financial statements and indicators

The ability to analyze and understand financial statements can be a valuable skill for sales professionals. If you understand and know how to use the information contained in financial statements, you will be able to act effectively for your customers and for yourself.

Financial statements and indicators help to eliminate guesswork and provide a solid basis for decision-making. Here it's useful to understand:

- Financial statements, such as *balance sheets, profit-and-loss statements, financial budgets, sales reports,* and *operating results.*
- Financial indicators, such as *contribution margin, profit contribution, discounted cash flow, accounting rate of return,* and *investment risk.*
- Financial ratios, such as *current ratio, net profit to net worth, net profit to net sales.*

CUSTOMER FINANCIALS

Understanding your customer's financial situation is essential to the sales-planning process. If you can identify your customer's "bottom line" needs, you can link your product to these needs.

Consider your product within the context of reducing your customer's costs — including labour, work flow processing, materials, manufacturing, or distribution. Consider, too, how your product can help to improve your customer's revenues and meet "top line" goals. Either way, you have an opportunity to sell improved profits to your customer.

YOUR COMPANY FINANCIALS

It is equally important for you to understand the financial environment of your own company. This allows you to identify opportunities for improvement within your area of responsibility. Read and analyze your company's financial and sales reports. Know the financial basics of your company's products and services including:

- list pricing;
- cost structure;
- cost of sales; and
- gross margins.

Understand the factors that can affect the cost of your products, such as changes in supply and demand, the price of raw materials, and labour disruptions.

Your company's financial environment will also affect the kinds of terms or financing you can offer your customers. (We'll take a more detailed look at these financial issues in Part 4: Strategic Selling Skills.)

YOUR FINANCIALS

You should always keep on top of your personal financial circumstances, needs, and goals. (See Chapter 8: Setting Goals.) Sales professionals are compensated in various ways and according to different performance standards, so you should first understand your pay structure and all of its components: salary, commission, draw, expenses, etc.

Determine ways that you can maximize your compensation. Remember to investigate any opportunities within Canadian tax law.

Invest in appropriate insurance to safeguard your assets and income. This includes liability insurance, disability insurance, life insurance, and automobile insurance.

SUMMARY

1. Business knowledge comprises product knowledge, an understanding of your industry's regulatory and legal framework, as well as financial knowledge.

2. Product knowledge includes understanding the technical details of what you sell, how they compare to those of your competitors, and how they are linked to your customers' needs.

3. Financial knowledge requires familiarity with various financial statements and indicators as they pertain to your customer, your own company, and to you personally.

Professional Development

As a sales professional, you are in the business of providing professional services to your employer. Successful sales representatives recognize the importance of developing and maintaining a professional standard of service, behaviour, and conduct in all areas of their work. This includes the way we act when representing our employer, and pertains also to our conduct with our peers, competitors, and customers.

ETHICAL CONDUCT

The issue of ethical conduct is central to the practice of consultative selling. As a sales professional, and a representative of your employer, it is critical that you behave ethically.

Let's consider some of the fundamental rules of ethical sales practice.

DECLARE CONFLICTS OF INTEREST

At some point, you may find yourself in a conflict of interest. For example, you may be working on orders from competing companies, or you may become involved in a situation where your personal interests conflict with your professional obligations. In these cases, it is critical that you declare a conflict of interest. To continue to act when your interests and motives are not clear is unethical behaviour.

MAINTAIN CONFIDENTIALITY

Whether it involves your employer or your customers, you have a responsibility to maintain confidentiality at all times. You are entrusted with vast quantities of sensitive data from both sources — including financial information, trade information, and personal information. "Entrusted" is the key word — you are obliged to fulfill and maintain that trust.

The CPSA Sales Institute

hereby certifies that

_____

having successfully completed the requirements for certification is upon the recommendation of the Board admitted to the status of

Certified Professional Sales Representative

and is entitled to all the honours, rights and privileges thereof.
Given under the seal of the CPSA Sales Institute

General Manager
CPSA Sales Institute

President
Canadian Professional Sales Association

Charter Member

Chairman of the Board
CPSA Sales Institute

Code of Ethics

The CPSA Sales Institute Code of Ethics is the set of principles and standards that a certified sales professional will strive to adhere to with *customers, organizations, competition, communities and colleagues.*

The certified professional pledges and commits to uphold these standards in all activities.

I will:

1. Maintain honesty and integrity in all relationships with *customers, prospective customers, and colleagues* and continually work to earn their trust and respect.

2. Accurately represent my products or services to the best of my ability in a manner that places my *customer or prospective customer* and my company in a position that benefits both.

3. Respect and protect the proprietary and confidential information entrusted to me by my company and my *customers* and not engage in activities that may conflict with the best interests of my *customers* or my company.

4. Continually upgrade my knowledge of my products/services, skills and my industry.

5. Use the time and resources available to me only for legitimate business purposes. I will only participate in activities that are ethical and legal, and when in doubt, I will seek counsel.

6. Respect my competitors and their products and services in a manner which is honest, truthful and based on accurate information that has been substantiated.

7. Endeavor to engage in business and selling practices which contribute to a positive relationship with the community.

8. Assist and counsel my fellow sales professionals where possible in the performance of their duties.

9. Abide by and encourage others to adhere to this Code of Ethics.

As a certified sales professional, I understand that the reputation and professionalism of all salespeople depends on me as well as others engaged in the sales profession, and I will adhere to these standards to strengthen the reputation and integrity for which we all strive. I understand that failure to consistently act according to this Code of Ethics may result in the loss of the privilege of using my professional sales designation.

HONOUR YOUR COMMITMENTS

A cornerstone of ethical practice is that you are as good as your word. If you have committed to something, then you should deliver it. This includes time frames, deliverables, service levels, quality, and warranties. You should also understand your customer's code of ethics and conduct yourself accordingly.

DEAL FAIRLY WITH COMPETITORS

As with customers and peers, salespeople are expected to behave ethically when dealing with competitors.

You can ethically monitor and analyze your competitors. Keep a competitive intelligence file where you compile information about your competitors' products, market share, and position, and any other pertinent information. Understand the implications of your competitors' activities and how they will affect your market. Be aware of your rights, and your competitors' rights in the market — including the rights of franchises.

Explore areas of common interest with your competitors to develop your relationship with them. Public service, through your local chamber of commerce or other business and service associations, provides a positive and neutral ground upon which you can interact with competitors and develop your understanding of them.

MANAGING YOUR PROFESSIONAL DEVELOPMENT

The Japanese use the word *kaizan* to describe the nature of the global marketplace. It means "a state of constant change and evolution." It accurately reflects the reality of today's world — with its advancing technologies, changing needs, and changing perspectives. In order to be successful in this environment, we need to evolve along with our changing marketplace. This requires a constant commitment to professional development.

Taking stock of yourself

Managing your professional development starts with an assessment of where you are now. Take a realistic inventory of your personal assets and current opportunities.

Think Globally, Act Locally

As a salesperson you manage a portion of your employer's business — a territory, a product line, or customer base. It is important for you to remember that you are part of a larger business and a larger marketplace. For many of us, the work we do is performed locally. Yet we are all part of a larger, global marketplace where our local actions reflect not only our image but that of our employer. It only makes sense, therefore, to bring a global perspective to our work on a local level. There are a number of ways to develop global perspective.

- **Identify the global reach of your organization.** Learn about the countries, markets, and customers with which your firm currently (or potentially) conducts business.

- **Investigate the global reach of your customers.** Familiarize yourself with your customers' customers and their markets. Develop an awareness of the political, economic, social, and technological culture of the countries involved. When you are dealing with customers or peers from another country, make the effort to understand them and follow appropriate business etiquette.

- **Understand the relevant international legal issues** such as copyright protocol, and excise and tax legislation. Your business in other countries will involve financial transactions, so you should develop an understanding of international financing and currency. Adapt your sales process, presentation, and communication style to the culture, country, or company with which you are doing business.

- **Consider learning another language** that will benefit the way you and your company do business. Join an export or industry association.

- **Keep in contact with other sales representatives** from your company who are serving your customer in other markets (that is, in the case of multinational or global industries).

- **Investigate international associations.** These can be a valuable source of contacts and information.

- **Be proactive in a global environment.** Identify new products/services and opportunities from new markets and communicate these opportunities to your company.

YOUR PERSONAL INVENTORY

- What are your personal interests?
- What are your notable skills and abilities?
- In what activities do you excel?
- What are your key areas of knowledge and understanding?

YOUR PROFESSIONAL INVENTORY

- Assess your level of competency in your current job. Where do you excel? In what areas do you require further skill development? (Use available self-assessment tools, and ask for feedback from colleagues/peers.)
- How do you rate yourself on the personality traits necessary for success?
- Investigate all aspects of your current job. Are there areas in which you can identify new opportunities for development? Can you link your strengths to new opportunities? Can you identify areas in which professional development will enhance your opportunities?

Creating a plan

Once you have taken inventory, you are ready to create a plan for your professional development. Recall how, in Chapter 8, we learned how to design a professional development plan for reaching your goals. Briefly, this plan consists of the following steps.

- Identify where you want to be (your next desired step).
- Identify the competency requirements for your future job.
- Create a personal growth strategy that supports your desired career path. Make an investment in moving towards the career goals you wish to reach. This can include applicable courses, seminars, and self-directed learning.
- Set personal goals and time frames for achieving them.

Managing your career path

Most successful people share the ability to managing their careers on an ongoing basis. This means setting career goals and maintaining a continual effort to attain those goals. Start by asking yourself what those goals are. In other words, where do you want go? How do you want your current work situation to change? Where do you want to be in five years?

◄█ Defining your career goals

Create a list of specific companies you would like to join, or product lines you are interested in selling, or specific jobs in which you are interested. It's a good idea to talk to people currently working in the type of position — or selling the kind of product line — that interests you. Conduct interviews with key people who are experienced in your area (or position) of interest. Find out what the job is really like and if it is really where you want to be. Conducting such interviews can help you to clarify how you can reach your goal. What are the expectations of that position or that company in terms of experience, education, and attitude?

> **Quotable...**
>
> *"Give me a stock clerk with a goal, and I will give you a man who will make history. Give me a man without a goal, and I will give you a stock clerk."*
>
> – J.C.Penney
> Zig Ziglar's Favorite Quotations. 1992

◄█ Creating your career plan

Your career plan should set out the series of steps that will take you towards your desired career goals. (Chapter 8 explains this process in detail.) In setting out your career plan, remember to consider your professional development goals. Continued development will be an important factor in reaching your desired outcomes. Link professional development to your career plan, setting concrete goals with time-bound completion dates.

Be realistic about the effort, development, and tasks that will be required to reach the next step of your career plan. Identify what you are prepared to do to get the next job on your path. Make specific goals which balance your commitment with the requirements needed to achieve the next step.

Is Your Resume Ready?

You never know when opportunity may present itself. Keep your resume current. Make sure it includes any community or association work you do, and lists your latest achievements in your professional life. Keeping your resume current also helps you to identify where professional development could round out your experience.

Outline specific, time-bound steps to reach that goal. Write them down and honour them. Refer to your career plan often and work on it in the same way you work towards all goals — that is, identify the steps required to reach the next step in your plan, write the steps down, schedule completion dates for each step using a time-management system, schedule the time necessary to complete each task, and act on your career plan.

Creating an environment for development

In addition to a personal plan for development, it is important to create an environment that facilitates ongoing self-improvement. Consider the following strategies:

- **Practise self-directed learning** using audio tapes, video tapes, and books. This will help you to develop those areas in your personal and professional inventory where you have identified a need to strengthen your skills. You can practise key skills on a regular basis by making this part of your weekly schedule.

- **Make note of any problems or mistakes** in the day-to-day performance of your job, and develop strategies to correct them. Identify the skills you can develop in order to prevent a problem from happening again.

- **Interact with your peers on a professional level.** This is an important tool for development and supports an environment of continual enrichment. Strategies to create this interaction include finding a mentor or being a mentor. Invest the time to become actively involved in professional associations like the Canadian Professional Sales Association (CPSA), customer-affiliated associations, or industry-specific associations. They are an invaluable source of information. They provide access to appropriate courses and seminars as well as to people who can support your continued development.

- **Acquire and understand up-to-date technical knowledge and tools.** This is a key factor in professional development and advancement, since the tools we use to conduct our business are constantly changing and advancing. Investing in the proper sales tools is a smart way to keep ahead in your career.

- **Keep informed about the latest technological advances,** and learn how you can use these technologies to enhance your work. Investigate the sales tools your competitors and peers are using to support their work. Effective salespeople learn to use all the resources and tools at their disposal — including computers, faxes, and voice-mail — to manage their time and efforts better. In particular, it is important to understand software products and their potential application to sales. The right software or hardware can make an important difference in the way you perform your job.

- **Pay attention to your personal health.** Managing your health is critical in all aspects of your life and affects your ability to do your job. Make sure you set personal health and wellness goals as part of your total goal-setting plan. Our lives need to be in balance if we wish to succeed.

SUMMARY

1. In order to be successful, salespeople must maintain professional standards in their work, and keep developing these standards on an ongoing basis.

2. Salespeople are expected to behave ethically.

3. Key elements of ethical behaviour include:
   - declaring conflicts of interest;
   - maintaining confidentiality;
   - honouring your commitments; and
   - dealing fairly with competitors.

4. In today's business environment it is increasingly important for you to "think globally, act locally."

5. Change is the one constant in today's marketplace. To keep up and be prepared, you need a strategy for professional development and career management.

Review: Self-management skills

1. The self-management skills discussed in Part 3 are a logical extension of our discussion in Part 1, where we looked at the key personality traits associated with successful people. Here we examined the skills necessary to develop those key traits.

2. Sales success depends on maintaining a positive attitude. Attitude is a product of personal self-talk. By changing your negative self-talk to positive self-talk, you improve your prospects for success.

3. Setting and maintaining goals is also a key factor in sales success. To be effective, goals must be S.M.A.R.T. (*Specific, Measurable, Achievable, Realistic,* and *Time-bound*).

4. Effective time management can help salespeople become more efficient and successful in their jobs. You can assess whether you are a good or poor time manager, and implement several strategies for ensuring deadlines and responsibilities are met promptly. Consider the monetary value of your time in order to make profitable time-allocation decisions.

5. Stress is a double-edged sword: we require stress in order to survive, but too much of it can kill us — literally. We can measure our relative stress levels using the stress index. There are a number of specific methods for managing the personal stress in our lives.

6. The ability to develop business knowledge is an important self-management skill, and it is critical for sales success. Business knowledge requires a thorough understanding of your products or services (and those of your competitors), as well as legal and financial issues pertaining to your business.

7. All salespeople should strive for the highest possible professional standards. You should adhere to the code of ethical conduct set out by the CPSA Sales Institute. Also, to keep pace with a constantly changing business environment, you should develop plans for professional development and career management.

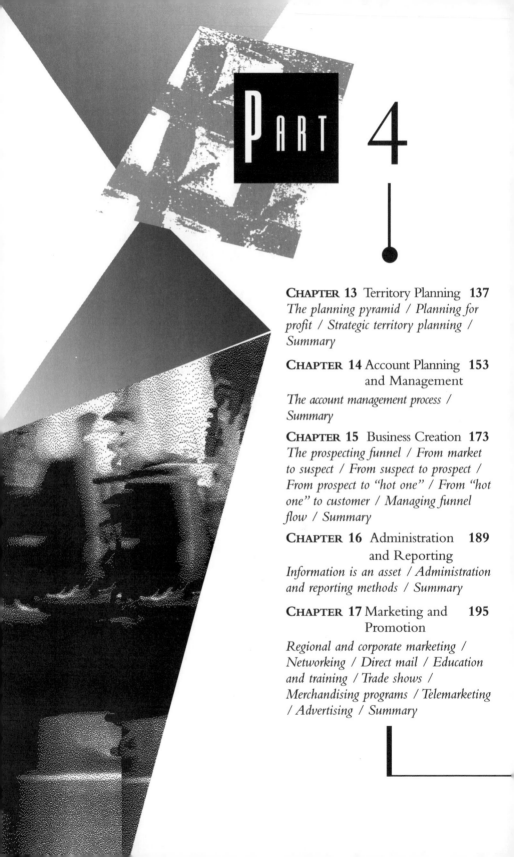

STRATEGIC SELLING SKILLS

Business success demands good products and services. It requires hard-working people. But these days, you need more. In the increasingly dynamic, competitive, and aggressive world of Canadian business, it is the strategic thinkers who get ahead.

In boom times, just about any hard-working, well intentioned sales representative can succeed if he or she has the necessary tactical and self-management skills. In a tougher economic climate, however, you can't get by on these qualities alone. You need to become a superior strategist, striving to get the most out of every available selling hour.

As a sales representative you have a formidable responsibility — that of managing a portion of your employer's business. It's up to you to maximize sales, customer satisfaction, and profitability.

Recall from Chapter 12 our reference to the phrase "Think globally, act locally" — originally coined by pioneer environmentalist René Dubos. Although he wasn't referring to strategic account management at the time, his comment is nevertheless applicable to our subject. As a sales professional, you benefit from constantly considering the "big picture"—looking down on your territory from above, in order to make decisions ("think globally") about how to invest your available selling time. You can also benefit from generating individual account goals, expectations, plans, and strategies ("act locally") to manage your territory on a "micro" level.

In order to apply this principle, you need to take a strategic approach to both (global and local) planes of activity. This means creating comprehensive goals, strategies, and action plans on many different levels. It also means striving to master the demands of your responsibilities within the constraints of time available. In addition, you need to employ strategic efforts in marketing and promotion to generate new business opportunities. Part 4 of this book examines these concepts and skills, along with others that can help you become more strategic, and therefore more successful.

Territory Planning

The strategic skills involved in territory planning are those directed to the "big picture." This type of planning requires setting overall goals for your territory and developing strategies for achieving those goals.

There are many factors to be considered in this process. Here we'll look at how territory planning fits into the process of organizational planning and management as a whole. Then, we'll discuss the importance of profitability to strategic planning, and provide you with specific sales tools for measuring and managing profitability or return on investment. We'll also revisit the topic of goal setting (first discussed in Chapter 8) within the context of successful territory management, and look at how you can create effective, strategic territory plans.

It should be noted that in some cases, the order or sequence of the steps involved in strategic territory planning can vary. For example, in some cases it may be more appropriate to set goals and objectives after conducting a thorough analysis. It's up to you and your sales manager to determine the most appropriate methodology. However, the approach we take here — as endorsed by the CPSA Sales Institute — is considered an acceptable standard.

By completing this chapter you will gain a better understanding of the competitive dynamics within your own territory. You will also develop a series of specific territory goals and a specific time frame for achieving them. This lays some of the foundation for developing a comprehensive, strategic territory plan to help you maximize profitability — and your own success.

THE PLANNING PYRAMID

Strategic planning takes place on many levels. The planning that you undertake as a sales representative represents only one part (although an important one) of a larger whole. This structure is represented in the *planning pyramid*, shown below.

Starting at the bottom or foundation, we see that the *strategic business plan* serves as the basis for all other planning within the organization. From this plan, an organization will develop departmental or divisional strategies — typically a *marketing plan*. Specific team plans follow, such as a *sales plan*. We continue up the pyramid until planning reaches the level of the individual employee. For sales representatives, this begins with a *territory plan* and eventually leads to individual *call planning*.

While the pyramid model is necessarily hierarchical, no single level is more important than any other. All levels are interdependent — they rely on one another, with each based on previous levels and representing the sum of the planning underlying it. For example, the marketing

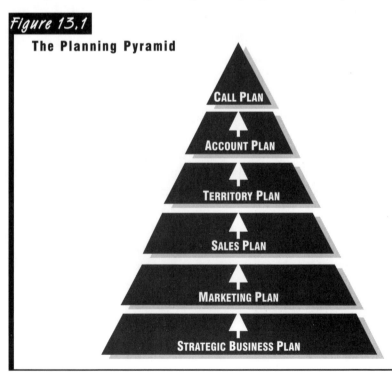

Figure 13.1

The Planning Pyramid

CALL PLAN

ACCOUNT PLAN

TERRITORY PLAN

SALES PLAN

MARKETING PLAN

STRATEGIC BUSINESS PLAN

This is a graphical representation of one possible schema for the various levels of planning within an organization.

plan encompasses the ideas, goals, and direction outlined in the strategic business plan. It is also the sum of all the relevant team plans (the sales plan). In this and following chapters, we will be looking at the levels that involve individual sales planning: the *territory plan*, *account plan*, and *call plan*.

PLANNING FOR PROFIT

Traditionally, there was only one real measure of a salesperson's performance — sales volume. So the goal of any plan was to increase sales. Today things are different. Sales volume is still important, but it's the *profitability* of those sales that really counts. For most salespeople — particularly those with a few years' experience — this new focus requires a change in thinking.

In the past you may have been encouraged to sell, sell, sell (*"Get out there and move product!"*). But chances are you're now being asked (or will be in the future) to adopt a more sophisticated approach: *"O.K. team, so let's get out there and maximize territory returns! Don't just sell volume — let's make our accounts more profitable and get significant sales growth — let's maximize return on every transaction."*

So how do you maximize those profits? The first step is to approach each sale focused on its profitability. The next is to to understand the financial elements upon which that profitability is based.

Take a look at Figure 13.2 (on the following page), which illustrates a simplified *income statement* for a fictitious company. As you can see, the bottom line comes down to the formula: *Sales − Costs = Profit.*

If you wish to improve profitability, it helps to think of your business in terms of the total equation. On the revenue side, look at selling prices and quantities sold. On the expense side, look at the costs associated with each transaction. Cost examples include items such as the time invested to get the sale, samples given, travel costs, and long-distance charges. Becoming aware of these factors and controlling them is essential to maximizing return.

Of course, there may be some factors that lie outside your control. Selling prices may be fixed, for example, or you may have no travel or sample costs. But just about everyone has control over the time they invest in each of their existing and prospective accounts.

Figure 13.2

Income Statements For Widgets & Repair Corp.

XYZ WIDGETS & REPAIR CORPORATION

INCOME STATEMENT
for the period ending December 31

Sales Revenues	$20,725
Cost of Goods Sold	12,435
GROSS PROFIT (MARGIN)	8,290

Selling & Administrative Expenses:

Selling Expenses	4,250	
Administrative Expenses	3,315	
Total Selling & Administrative Expenses		7,565
INCOME FROM OPERATIONS		725
Income Taxes		145
NET INCOME		$ 580

An income statement provides a summary of the profit performance of an entity over a given time period. The entity could be a private company, a division of a multi-national corporation, a sales region for an organization, a sales territory, or even a single product. All values are recorded in dollars and represent cumulative totals for the period in question. The income statement is designed to be read in a step-down manner. *Sales* (or revenues) are located at the top; *costs* (or expenses) are subtracted as you proceed down the statement. *Profit* (or net income) is located at the bottom of the statement, indicated by a double underline.

Return on time invested (R.O.T.I.)

As a salesperson with limited time available, you need to decide how to invest that time in the most productive (or profitable) way possible. You can do this by employing a mathematical formula that measures the return you get on time invested. This formula is known as *return on time invested*, or by its acronym, R.O.T.I. — a productivity ratio that is calculated as follows:

$$\text{Return on Time Invested (R.O.T.I.)} = \frac{\text{Gross Profit (GP)}}{\text{Time (T) required to capture GP}}$$

In cases where the gross profit cannot be determined (for example, where product costing information is unavailable), you can substitute gross sales. In this case, R.O.T.I. ratios will be relatively higher, but just as valuable for profitability decision-making.

PUTTING R.O.T.I. TO WORK

So how can you use this R.O.T.I. information to improve profitability? Here are a few suggestions;

1. Set minimum R.O.T.I. standards on a daily, weekly, or monthly basis for
   - your overall territory;
   - existing accounts, new accounts, and prospective accounts;
   - big accounts, medium accounts, and small accounts;
   - accounts in certain geographical areas; and
   - individual product lines.

2. Manage current customer relationships in order to maximize R.O.T.I. Look for ways to reduce time spent on the account or increase sales volume in the same amount of selling time. Alternatively, look for opportunities to improve selling prices.

3. Maximize R.O.T.I. with each new or prospective customer. Determine minimum selling prices based on desired R.O.T.I. and the time required to secure the customer. Or, in competitive pricing situations, establish the amount of time available to secure the customer, based on minimum expected R.O.T.I.

4. Determine which prospects offer the best financial viability. Some opportunities may not yield a desirable R.O.T.I. — possibly because they require too much time to secure and maintain a small volume of business or because they are demanding too low a price.

In Practice

Let's say that you have a customer who has contributed $12,000 gross profit over the past year, and the time required to service the account is approximately 2 hours per month. What is the R.O.T.I. ratio of this account?

$$\text{Return on Time Invested (R.O.T.I.)} = \frac{\$12,000}{2 \text{ hrs/month X 12 months}}$$

$$= \frac{\$12,000}{24}$$

$$= 500$$

5. Constantly ask yourself: "How is what I'm doing right now directly tied to revenue generation, and how is it helping me to improve my R.O.T.I. or profitability?"

Regardless of the methodology, maximizing profitability is a significant goal of today's sales professional. The philosophy of merely increasing sales volume isn't sufficient. And the R.O.T.I ratio is a valuable tool for achieving this new goal.

◄█ Setting profit goals

Improving profitability on your sales won't happen by itself. You need to define specific profit goals.

> **Quotable...**
> *"A man without a purpose is like a ship without a rudder."*
> −THOMAS CARLYLE
> Scottish historian and philosopher, 1795-1881

As you'll recall from Chapter 8, goals must meet certain criteria in order to be effective. We grouped these criteria under the acronym S.M.A.R.T. (*Specific, Measurable, Achievable, Realistic,* and *Time-bound*). Let's revisit those criteria in the context of setting profit goals.

Specific. It is not enough to establish a sales objective such as: *increase sales of product X by 50%.* Effective goals should provide more detail, such as: *obtain a 50% increase in sales of Product X with a 25% profit margin through 10% growth in new business; securing 15 competitors' customers through strong product performance and demonstrations; and a 25% growth within existing accounts through new product applications.*

Measurable. How close are you to achieving your profit goal? In order to know this, the goal must be measurable. For example: *obtain 25 new customers during the next quarter or increase sales of product X by 10% to existing customers over the next six months while maintaining a return of at least 30%.*

Achievable. Effective goals are attainable. There's no point to setting your goal as: *increase sales and profitability by 100% within the next year.* Much better to set targets of, say, *10% growth per quarter.* If you find subsequently that this goal is too modest, you can always revise it upward.

Realistic. Effective goals are realistic. They embrace the organization's culture, values, and vision. If your goals are not realistic, they won't be attainable and may actually impede territory planning.

Time-bound. If specific completion dates are not identified, goals

Objectives at Work

The value of having defined goals and objectives can be seen in the well-known business model *Management By Objectives (MBO)*. In this model employees establish a series of performance objectives together with their managers. The employee is then held accountable for achieving those objectives. Objectives usually embrace a relatively short time frame and are, therefore, revised often. All performance goals and objectives are usually outlined in writing; copies are retained by both the employee and supervisor. This management model often proves effective, based on its methodical use of goal setting practices to optimize performance.

can become wish lists rather than specific definitions of intended performance. An example of a time-bound goal would be: *obtain 25 new customers before December 31 of this year.*

SETTING COMPATIBLE GOALS

Territory planning consists of two distinct types of goals: *overall territory objectives* and *individual account targets*. Overall territory objectives are typically established first. Individual account targets are determined next. (Taken together, these targets make up your territory objectives.)

Here it makes sense to ensure that both types of goals are compatible — that they are aimed at achieving a unified purpose and are consistent with planning levels outlined in the planning pyramid discussed earlier.

How do you ensure your goals are compatible? Start by taking the time to read all internal publications that deal with corporate objectives and plans. In addition, you should usually set your goals in consultation with your manager. Review corporate objectives and plans, ask questions to check your understanding, and discuss the role your goals play as part of the overall plan. Once sales objectives and performance expectations are mutually developed, accepted, and understood, they should be documented.

PREVIOUS PERFORMANCE AND MISSED OPPORTUNITIES

When you're setting profit goals and developing plans for existing accounts, review the history of each account, looking for any missed opportunities. Current goals and plans can then be developed accordingly.

STRATEGIC TERRITORY PLANNING

Once you've established your territory goals and objectives, the next step is to define specific strategies or plans to achieve those targets. Strategic territory planning involves analyzing your territory on a global level — not account by account (that will come later), but based on broad, general considerations.

Here you can analyze your territory using an assessment model known as S.W.O.T. This describes the *Strengths*, *Weaknesses*, *Opportunities*, and *Threats* within your territory on three levels — *the competition, the marketplace,* and *your organization.* The results of a S.W.O.T. analysis can be organized into a chart similar to that shown on page 145, where the data can be reviewed on a single page.

Within each quadrant of the chart, consider the various elements in terms of how you can increase profitability. For example, the top-right cell of Figure 13.3 asks you to identify and analyze the specific strengths of the marketplace. These strengths might include a general uptrend in the number of potential customers for your product, or a specific opportunity arising from the development of a new application for your product. (Note that different cells in the S.W.O.T. analysis may identify the same issues; in some cases this is unavoidable, although it may indicate situations requiring the salesperson's special attention.)

The S.W.O.T. analysis calls upon you to analyze your entire target market (the market defined by your sales territory). As part of this analysis, some other things to consider are:

- key contacts in the marketplace;
- the overall level of satisfaction of your customers and the marketplace in general;
- market demographics;
- the future of the marketplace (what/who will remain the same, what/who will grow, etc.);
- your percentage of market share; and
- the ratio between sales dollars and the number of current customers/prospective customers.

The goal of the S.W.O.T. analysis is to gain an "overhead view" of your territory as a whole in order to design strategies for improvement. Following this initial analysis, there's one critical element that warrants more detailed scrutiny — *the competition.*

Figure

Model of A S.W.O.T. Analysis Used for Strategic Territory Planning

	YOUR ORGANIZATION	THE COMPETITION	THE MARKETPLACE
S STRENGTHS	your organization's specific strengths in the marketplace (products, the sales and/or service process, the company itself, etc.)	the competition's specific strengths in the marketplace	specific marketplace strengths that can help in your effort to maximize profits (expanding target market, new applications or sales channels, etc.)
W WEAKNESSES	your organization's specific weaknesses in the marketplace (non-competitive pricing strategies, non-compliance with industry standard, etc.)	the competition's specific weaknesses in the marketplace	specific marketplace weaknesses that can help or hinder your ability to maximize profitability
O OPPORTUNITIES	specific opportunities that exist within your organization to help you maximize return (new applications or customers or needs, etc.)	specific opportunities you face concerning your competition, regarding your ability to maximize profits	specific marketplace opportunities that can be capitalized on to maximize return (new applications or sales channels, etc.)
T THREATS	specific things, people, or circumstances within your organization that threaten your ability to maximize profits	specific threats you face from your competition in your efforts to maximize return	specific marketplace considerations that pose a threat to your ability to maximize profits

The S.W.O.T. analysis examines the strengths, weaknesses, opportunities, and threats faced by sales representatives in their entire territory on three different levels (the competition, the marketplace, and their own company). Factors in each quadrant are examined, relative to their ability to help or hinder profit-maximization efforts.

Competitive analysis

Your competition is perhaps one of the main sources of opportunity and difficulty in your territory. So it makes sense to examine your competition thoroughly. Who poses the greatest or least threat? What is the source of their strengths and weaknesses? Which competitors require some action on your part? How you can overcome threats posed by competitors — and how can you become an even bigger threat to them? These are some of the questions that need to be answered by an in-depth competitive analysis.

ESTABLISHING CRITERIA FOR ANALYSIS

Start your competitive analysis by preparing a list of the criteria that will identify your primary competitors. Which factors are most important? Market share will certainly be one criterion. Others may include price, quality, turnaround time, service, advertising, and training. (As you might expect, the list will vary from industry to industry and company to company.)

Take a few minutes to consider what the list should be for your organization. How should you assess the competition? Criteria may include:

- products
- literature
- pricing
- sales processes
- service
- packaging
- delivery
- quality
- size of company
- market share

- financial picture
- experience within the industry
- skill and expertise of sales force
- effectiveness of the sales force
- advertising
- distribution systems
- human resources and training
- proximity to customer base

Once you have determined your list of criteria, assign a relative importance to each based on the customer's perspective. Rate each criterion on a scale of 1 through 10 (10 being extremely important to customers, 1 being relatively unimportant to customers).

IDENTIFYING AND RATING COMPETITORS

Once you have identified the principal criteria upon which to assess your competitors, it's time to analyze and rate them based on their relative strength of performance. The performance rating scale is between 1 and 10 (where 10 is the best and 1 is the worst performance.)

Before you rate each of your competitors, however, first gather as much information as possible on each one. Some of the strategies you might employ to collect competitive information include:

- reading annual reports, trade magazines, or industry publications;
- networking with the competition;
- mystery shopping the competition;
- asking customers about the competition; and
- visiting competitors' booths at trade shows.

Use a chart similar to that shown below to assemble the ratings data from this analysis. Expand the chart (in width or depth) as necessary to accommodate the criteria and competitors involved.

CRITERION	RELATIVE IMPORTANCE	YOUR COMPANY	COMPETITOR #1	COMPETITOR #2	COMPETITOR #3	COMPETITOR #4
1.						
2.						
3.						
4.						
5.						

COMPLETING YOUR ANALYSIS

When all of your competitors have been rated, the results can be analyzed. Use a four-quadrant chart like the one shown below to analyze each competitor — use one chart per organization. Record the criteria for measur-

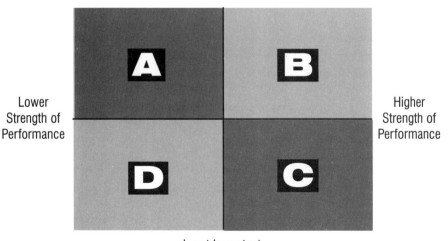

Most Important
Selection Criteria

Lower
Strength of
Performance

Higher
Strength of
Performance

Least Important
Selection Criteria

Figure 13.4

Competitive Analysis Scoring Key

Most Important
Selection Criteria

Lower
Strength of
Performance

Higher
Strength of
Performance

A
Criteria that are very
important and represent
firm's weaknesses

B
Criteria that are very
important and represent
firm's strengths

D
Criteria that are least
important and represent
firm's weaknesses

C
Criteria that are least
important and represent
firm's strengths

Least Important
Selection Criteria

CELL A - "SERIOUS PROBLEMS"
For your organization, any criteria that are in this cell represent serious weaknesses. You must work to improve these factors if you are going to have a competitive offering in the marketplace. Any of your competitors whose criteria fall in this cell represent opportunities for you to attack and capitalize upon.

CELL B - "KEEP UP THE GOOD WORK"
For both your organization and the competition, this cell represents strengths. More importantly, these are relative strengths that are appreciated by customers. If this cell is "void" for any firm in a given segment, it really does not have a true competitive differential. It is marginal in terms of meeting the needs of the marketplace.

CELL C - "WHY BOTHER"
The marketplace does not value these criteria even though they represent strengths to these firms. Unless the importance of these criteria can be increased or there are other markets that value these things, they are phantom strengths. They do not create a differential advantage and may turn off clients if you try to sell them. Moreover, they usually require resources to maintain. Have you ever been approached by a seller who kept talking about features or benefits that were of little interest to you?

CELL D - "NEEDS WATCHING"
This cell is important only to the extent that you should not be spending time or resources to improve these factors. They may be a part of the total offering that has some value but they by no means create the differential. Make sure that your competitors are not educating customers to increase the importance of these criteria. You should continue to monitor changes to keep abreast of this possibility.

Scoring key adapted from *Be Your Own Sales Manager*, Tony Alessandra, Jim Cathcart, and John Monoky, © 1990.

ing competitors in the appropriate quadrants. The quadrant where you enter each criterion will depend on how the organization scored in the rating chart previously discussed. Don't forget to complete an analysis chart for your own organization to compare with the others.

Once a chart has been completed for each competitor (and your company), use the scoring key on page 148 to assess the results.

Allocating your selling time

The next step in strategic territory planning is to determine how you should allocate your available selling time to the various activities of business creation, existing account management, and administrative or other activities. This allocation will differ for each salesperson, reflecting variations in territories, organizations, industries, and marketplaces.

As you'll recall from previous chapters, a salesperson generally has 1,880 available working hours in a year. So you can use this figure to begin the apportionment of your selling time. Again, you should do this in close consultation with your sales manager to ensure that your time allocation corresponds to corporate plans, objectives, standards, and expectations.

Strategy development

Now you're ready to generate a comprehensive strategy for profit maximization — incorporating your goal setting, S.W.O.T. analysis, and competitive analysis. Your territory plan should cover a period no longer than one year and preferably only one business quarter (three months). State the goals to be achieved, along with specific steps or action plans to be undertaken. Each step should be time-bound and clearly tied to the achievement of at least one of the goals or objectives.

The written territory plan is an official document that should provide the following details:

- sales representative's name;
- sales territory involved;
- time period covered by the plan;
- specific goals and results expected;
- steps to be taken to achieve goals and results;
- specific time frames for completing action steps and achieving goals; and

- automatic checkpoints and interim objectives, which can be used to assess performance and progress towards overall goals.

You and your sales manager should each keep a copy of the territory plan for future review and performance assessment. Here are a few additional points to consider when developing your territory plan.

- Identify which selling activities will prove most profitable and plan to apportion your time accordingly between them — remember, you still have to do them all; the question is how much time you will dedicate to each activity.
- Identify specific market segments and treat each accordingly.
- Review the specific physical and geographic elements of your territory.
- Conduct research and identify new prospective customers, applications, markets, competitors, regulations, and industry developments.
- Identify new opportunities for cross-selling or up-selling within existing accounts.
- Review the centres of influence within existing business sectors.
- Analyze similar markets for comparison purposes.
- Identify the top 20% of your customer base and define specific account classifications (we'll take a detailed look at this process in the next chapter).
- Review selling prices, expenses, and overall profitability.

Be sure to dedicate significant time and thought to the development of a thorough territory plan — it serves as the basis for all other planning to be done, as we will see in the following chapters.

SUMMARY

1. Territory planning is the first step in the strategic planning process. It is important here to focus on profitability, not just sales volume. One way to do this is to maximize *return on time invested* (R.O.T.I.) at all times.

2. The first step in generating a strategic territory plan involves setting goals and objectives. These profit-oriented goals should be S.M.A.R.T. (*Specific, Measurable, Achievable, Realistic,* and *Timebound*).

3. A S.W.O.T. analysis helps to assess the *Strengths*, *Weaknesses*, *Opportunities*, and *Threats* as they relate to your organization, the competition, and the marketplace itself. Competitive analysis is particularly important.

4. Following your analyses, you need to decide (preferably with your sales manager) how to allocate the 1,880 working hours available to you each year.

5. The final step in territory planning is to develop a comprehensive strategy for managing your territory. There are a number of factors to be considered in this process, some of which will be more applicable to your situation than others.

Account Planning and Management

In the last chapter, we examined the importance and methodology of overall territory planning. There we saw that, in order to achieve territorial objectives and goals, it often makes sense to break the challenge up into smaller, more manageable pieces. Hence the importance of *account planning* — the next level up on the planning pyramid.

At the account level, there are essentially two ways to maximize profit growth within your sales territory: managing existing accounts toward improved returns; and, seeking out and securing new business. In Chapter 15: Business Creation, we'll look at the latter of those two components. Here, we'll be examining the often complex process of *account management*.

THE ACCOUNT MANAGEMENT PROCESS

Account management is a process that examines "living" account relationships. The relationship that you and your company have with a customer is dynamic — it is constantly changing and evolving. The people involved in buying decisions change, the customer's product needs evolve, financial stability changes (for better or worse), and so on. In this way, customer relationships mirror the ever-changing conditions of life itself. Hence the term *living* account relationships.

In this chapter, we'll be looking at account management as a cyclical, four-step process, where each step is designed to ensure maximum profitability for any given account. The cyclical character of the process is derived from the dynamic nature of the relationship with each customer. In other words, there is no beginning or end to the process. And, just like territory planning, it covers a finite period of time, requiring you to go through the process continually for each of your customers.

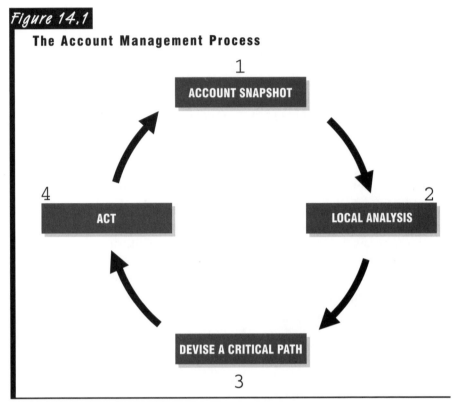

Figure 14.1

The Account Management Process

1
ACCOUNT SNAPSHOT

4
ACT

2
LOCAL ANALYSIS

DEVISE A CRITICAL PATH
3

This model illustrates the dynamic process of account management required by sales professionals today. It involves taking a "snapshot" of an account at a given moment in time, thoroughly analyzing that account on a local level, developing specific action plans to achieve defined goals, and acting on those plans.

As can be seen from Figure 14.1 above, account management starts with taking a "snapshot" of an account at a given moment in time. This is followed by a thorough analysis of the account on a local level. Next comes a specific action plan to achieve defined goals. Finally, you act on that plan. Steps 1 to 3 constitute account planning. The fourth step is the process of active management. Together they comprise account management.

Step 4 — *Act* — takes place over a specific period of time and is linked directly to the territory plan. In most cases, you'll need to perform account planning more often than territory planning. For example, if territory planning is done every six months, then account planning could be done on a quarterly basis. In other words, a "snapshot" would be taken of each customer every three months. This enables the account management process to serve as a check for territory planning, assessing progress towards territory and corporate objectives.

Once the period covered by the critical path has expired — or if there are significant changes with the account, within the representative's organization, or in the marketplace itself — the process begins anew by taking another snapshot.

Let's examine each component of the four-step account management process in detail, along with other relevant issues.

◂1 The snapshot

The process of gathering together all of the data available on your accounts is known as taking a snapshot. Here are some examples of the type of information you might want to assemble.

- your overall territory plan and support documentation;
- previous goals and account plans for each customer;
- customer or territory budgets;
- sales and other internal reports;
- each customer's buying history and patterns;
- published corporate missions, goals, strategies, and/or plans;
- relevant marketplace or industry publications;
- a complete customer listing, including full addresses; and
- any other available information.

It is from this information that you can analyse the current situation, set specific account goals, and generate a critical path for achieving those goals.

◂2 Local analysis

The second step in the account management process is to conduct a local analysis of each account. Here you examine an account on a micro level, looking at all the details of the account and each of the people who may have an impact on buying decisions. (We'll consider the role of these people, called *buying influences*, on the next few pages.)

A local analysis requires you to forecast the expected value of each customer over a given period of time, classifying your accounts according to their expected returns, and to allocate your available selling time accordingly. Local analysis is critical to the account management process and it is perhaps the most time-consuming step of all.

> ### Remember the Big Picture
>
> Before undertaking your local analysis, take a moment to review the results of the global analysis contained in your strategic *territory plan.* This will help to ensure that both levels of planning (global and local) are consistent and complementary. Constant reference to territory plans is important throughout the account management process.
>
> The global issues to consider include your strengths, weaknesses, opportunities, and threats on three levels — the competition, the marketplace, and your own organization — but *only as they relate to that account.* In other words, while it may not make sense to spend much time considering these issues as they relate to your territory, it is valuable to consider them as they relate to a specific account.

The primary function of this step in the account management process is to assemble the information that may prove valuable in developing a strategy to improve profitability at a given account. This process involves examining the specific details of each account, including all buying influences.

✓ *Personal Check*

Understanding the local issues

☐ The customer's buying history and patterns (buying cycle)

☐ Previous goals and account plans

☐ Previous performance and missed opportunities (see chapter 13)

☐ The nature of your customer's business

☐ The customer's products or services

☐ The customer's customers

☐ The customer's organizational structure

☐ The customer's financial position

☐ The customer's mission, vision, goals, plans, and major initiatives

☐ The competition's share of business at each account

☐ The specific benefits you can bring to the customer relationship

Once you have gathered all of the relevant data concerning these issues, it is valuable to conduct a close-up examination of the people involved at each account. At each of your current customers and prospective accounts, there may be several people who influence various buying decisions. These people are called buying influences. And as the size and importance of a sale increases, so does the likelihood that there will be more than one of them involved.

Who are the buying influences?

When an account has only one person who makes or influences the buying decision, your job is relatively straightforward. When several people are involved, however, account management can become more complex. By identifying these individuals (or *buying influences*) and the role they play in the decision-making process, you can improve your chances of building an appropriate strategy to penetrate the account. Therefore, when analyzing an account it is valuable to consider this information carefully.

In their renowned book, *Strategic Selling*^{SM}, Robert Miller and Stephen Heiman identified four roles buying influences can play within an organization. Three of these roles are illustrated below in Figure 14.2. The fourth role we will discuss independently (see box, page 159). Review the chart carefully and use the space in the "example" column to list individuals from several of your customers who play each role.

Figure 14.2

Buying Influence Roles

	IDENTIFYING CLUES	FOCUSES ON	ASKS	EXAMPLE
ECONOMIC BUYER	• Direct access to $ • Releases $ • The only one who can say *yes* • Has final veto power	• Bottom line • Impact on organization	*"What kind of return will we get on this investment?"*	
USER BUYER	• Using or supervising use of your product • Can say *no* • Can support you but can't say *yes*	• The job to be done	*"How will it work for me?"*	
TECHNICAL BUYER	• Assesses measurable & quantifiable data • Often the "Gatekeeper" • Gives advice • Can say no • Can support you but can't say *yes*	Your product	*"Does it meet the specs?"*	

Robert Miller and Stephen Heiman identified four buying roles individuals play within organizations. Three of these are outlined above: the Economic Buyer, the User Buyer, and the Technical Buyer. The chart describes clues for identifying each role, the focus each role maintains in the buying decision, and the types of questions each role considers. The buying role each person plays can change with each sale and in some cases individuals can play multiple roles.

Keep in mind that a person's role as a buying influence within an organization can change with each sale, even though his or her job title doesn't. In addition, individuals can play multiple roles or serve a single purpose. Thus, knowing who is playing which role calls for constant reassessment.

Let's take a closer look at the different buying influences identified by Miller and Heiman.

The Economic Buyer. One of the biggest challenges we face when dealing with multiple buying influences is finding the *economic buyer*. In every case, there is only one economic buyer and he or she is usually highly placed in the organization. Here are some of the factors that determine who plays the role of economic buyer:

- the value (dollar amount and perceived benefit) of the sale;
- the business conditions existing within the customer organization;
- the customer's experience with you and your organization;
- the customer's experience with your products or services; and
- the potential impact of the sale on the organization.

In many cases you may believe that your contact is with the economic buyer when it's actually not. People will often position themselves as having the ultimate decision, usually with statements like *"I have the final say on this project."* However, in many cases, these individuals are actually required to seek final approval from someone else in the organization — for example, their manager, the finance department, or the purchasing department.

The **User Buyer** and **Technical Buyer** can endorse or veto your proposal, but they can't say "yes." Only the economic buyer has that authority, and sometimes that person is difficult to identify or get to. Sometimes your contact will block your attempts to meet this ultimate buyer influence. In this event, focus your efforts on improving the relationship with the other influences. Demonstrate the value of meeting with the economic buyer — perhaps to help present the recommended proposal. Use your influencing skills to gain approval for a meeting.

Decisions, Decisions...

Do you know how the customer organization makes its buying decisions? If not, try asking questions to clarify how the process works, then modify your sales strategies and plans accordingly. Try creating a "war map" of strategies, moves, and countermeasures to manage the advancement of your proposal through the decision-making process.

Coach's Corner

The fourth buying influence role identified by Miller and Heiman (but not included in the chart on page 157) is called the *coach*. In today's competitive marketplace, with its demand for increasingly strategic sales management, having a coach for each account is critical.

Coaches focus on issues like: *"How can we make this work?"* Their primary goal is to help you in your selling efforts. They can provide and interpret information about various situations throughout the selling process, the buying influences involved, how each side of the sale wins, and the customer organization as a whole. Your coach's focus is on the success of your selling efforts. His or her goal is for you to win the business. Coaches provide advice, support, and guidance in your efforts to maximize profitability. They can be found in a number of places:

- **The customer's organization.** Some of the best coaches are those found in the customer's organization. These individuals can provide you with inside advice and guidance in your selling efforts. Often this type of coach is the person in the organization with whom you have had the longest relationship, or someone who is not involved in the actual sale you are pursuing.

- **Your own organization.** Often, coaches can be found in your own organization. They are usually able to provide you with strategic advice, based on personal experience and their knowledge of the customer organization (and their buying influences), the industry, the marketplace, your products, and/or your selling process. Frequently, this type of coach is a fellow sales representative or your sales manager.

- **Outside of both organizations.** Sometimes you are able to establish a coaching relationship with someone outside of both your and the customer's organization. These individuals may prove valuable because they can provide outside, impartial advice on your selling efforts. Their advice may be particularly helpful if they have personal experience with the customer organization (and the other buying influences), and/or the industry.

Remember that you can always have more than one coach. In fact, it's advantageous to have many — preferably one from each of the sources listed above for every customer.

In creating your local analysis, be sure to keep track of all the buying influences within each customer organization. Assemble all of the available information on each one, and write it down. (Again, remember that they may change from sale to sale.) Once this information has been gathered, analyze the situation. Indicate areas of threat or weakness with a warning sign like ✗.

Place a mark on the page next to the buying influences that represent problem areas. Then describe the details of the threat or weakness. These warning signs indicate buying influences that require your attention and will alert you when it comes time to complete the next step of the account management process — developing a critical path.

Listed below are some of the situations requiring the assignment of a graphic warning sign:

✗ a reorganization within the customer's organization;

✗ a lack of information about a specific influence;

✗ if you are unsure about something;

✗ any buying influence you have yet to contact;

✗ any buying influence who is new to his/her position; or

✗ any buying influence who is overconfident that your proposal isn't necessary.

Once you have analyzed the buying influences and decision-making process within each account, the next step of the local analysis involves forecasting account profitability.

MAKING YOUR FORECAST

Forecasting is a valuable component of your local analysis, especially since it may be used as a yardstick for measuring your performance.

Account forecasting (often called budgeting) is an informed prediction of how much a customer will buy over a given period of time. This prediction process is quite detailed, quantitative, and can be quite effective — particularly with practice and experience.

The process involves gathering all of the information for an account, including the results of the global analysis and assessment of the various buying influences. A detailed assessment of this information will enable you to determine the various selling activities that you expect to undertake with the customer. It may be useful to complete a chart similar to the *"What Am I Gonna Do At This Account"* assessment tool presented in Figure 14.3 below. This tool will help to summarize critical data for the balance of the forecasting process.

Figure 14.3

The "What Am I Gonna Do At This Account?" Assessment Tool

PROFIT BUILDING ACTIVITY	WHAT I'M GONNA DO
increasing the volume of current products	
introducing a new product line (side-selling or cross-selling)	
move up to a better product line (up-selling)	
adjust selling price	
expense management (samples, delivery, selling time, etc...)	

This tool helps representatives outline the profit generation activities they intend to undertake with a given account over a specified period of time. The tool lists the five main methods for profit generation within existing accounts and asks representatives to indicate what they intend to do in each area for that customer.

Once you've thoroughly assessed the available information, you'll need to quantify your forecast. The basic formula for this is provided in Figure 14.4 on page 162. Here you need to consider previous-period profitability, estimated profit growth and attrition for the current period, and customer-specific expenses that will be required. With these variables known, you can calculate an account's expected value and profitability.

In some cases, of course, you may not have access to information about profit margins on your products. Even so, forecasting can still be quite valuable. If you don't know the profit margin, use gross sales dollars instead. Your forecast of the expected value of the account will still serve as a tangible, quantifiable goal. And, assuming that you govern yourself with an eye towards profit maximization (not just sales volume increases), meeting these targets for each account will lead to overall territory growth and prosperity.

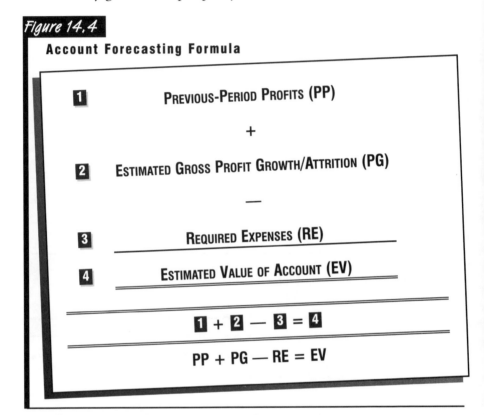

Figure 14.4

Account Forecasting Formula

[1]   PREVIOUS-PERIOD PROFITS **(PP)**

$+$

[2]   ESTIMATED GROSS PROFIT GROWTH/ATTRITION **(PG)**

$-$

[3]   REQUIRED EXPENSES **(RE)**

[4]   ESTIMATED VALUE OF ACCOUNT **(EV)**

[1] $+$ [2] $-$ [3] $=$ [4]

PP + PG — RE = EV

This is a basic formula for forecasting the expected profitability of a given customer over a specific period of time. In cases where profit margins are not known, total revenue may be substituted instead. This formula is much more complex than it may appear on the surface. Given the many variables involved, the calculation can become quite involved — especially concerning line #2 (estimated gross profit growth). Some of the issues to be considered are: the number of products involved, varying profit margins between each product or sale, the introduction of new products, the knowledge of product margins, competitive activity within the amount, the expected increase in product usage, and many more.

Let's examine the account forecasting formula on a line-by-line basis.

Previous-period profits (PP) are usually easy to determine; they are a matter of record.

Estimated gross profit growth/attrition (PG) can become quite a detailed calculation, however. A typical method for calculating PG is to determine the total amount of *usage* growth for each product line; then assess the probability (percentage) of securing that new volume, and multiply the expected growth by the rate to obtain a *realized* expected growth; then multiply the realized expected growth by the profit margin (percentage) for that product line to obtain the expected profit growth for that product; and finally, repeat this calculation for each product line. The sum of these calculations would yield a complex, yet accurate PG.

In some cases, this method for calculating estimated profit growth/attrition may be unrealistic. For example, selling prices (and therefore profit margins) may vary from sale to sale. In other situations, profit margins may be volatile because of significant fluctuations in product costs. Even so, estimating PG is the most critical element of the account forecasting formula and should be treated accordingly.

In making this calculation, be sure to consider all of the factors that can affect gross profit. Examples include:

- the results of your overall territory analysis and *territory plan*;
- the results of your *global analysis*;
- your *"What Am I Gonna Do At This Account?"* assessment tool results;
- profit margin variances between products;
- product cost volatility;
- selling price variances;
- the number of product lines involved;
- new product lines;
- market segmentation;
- competitive activity at the account and your ability to secure all usage growth;
- the business you may lose;
- customer usage fluctuations based on business cycles; and
- overall customer usage growth.

Required expenses (RE). Accounting for these expenses is relatively straightforward. It requires a simple estimation of any extra expenses required to secure and maintain the customer's business. In other words, you should consider only those expenses that are directly tied to an individual account. Other expenses — such as corporate overhead, management salaries, or research and development — are not involved (although some organizations use a flat overhead allocation when calculating overall territory profitability, in order to spread these types of expenses across the smallest business unit—a sales territory). Some of the expenses that you may wish to consider are:

- product samples;
- promotional materials;
- merchandising costs;
- co-op advertising;
- equipment loans;
- direct travel expenses;
- direct delivery or warehousing expenses; and
- extra selling time (recall the cost of your selling time, as discussed in Chapter 12).

As we've seen, the account forecasting formula can become quite complex. It requires you to consider all of the factors that affect account profitability.

Be sure to record your forecasted sales results as part of each account plan. Account forecasting is best done in conjunction with your manager. Talk to him or her to ensure that you're working within corporate targets. Ask questions to confirm your understanding, and discuss the role your goals play as part of the overall plan. Negotiate expectations and mutually agreeable financial targets for each account. Again, remember to make sure that your targets are S.M.A.R.T. (*Specific, Measurable, Achievable, Realistic,* and *Time-bound*).

CLASSIFYING YOUR ACCOUNTS

Clearly, all customers are not equal. Nor is the value they represent to you and your sales territory. So it makes sense to classify each of your accounts according to their forecasted value.

Here we can look to Vilfredo Pareto — an Italian economist, sociologist, and philosopher — who is known for "the 80/20 rule" or "the Pareto Principle." In a strategic selling context, it means that the top 20% of accounts in a sales territory should yield 80% of the profit for that territory. Of course, the actual numbers for your sales territory may not work out that way. But the top 20% of your accounts will probably generate a significant portion of your territory's revenue.

The principle of account classification is based on the assumption that customers deserve varying amounts of your selling time, based on the return they bring to you and your territory. Recall our discussion of profitability and R.O.T.I. (return on time invested) from Cchapter 12. Given that maximizing profit depends on how you allocate your time, it follows that you must be able to classify your accounts according to their expected profitability.

There are many methods available for classifying accounts. One of the most widely used (and the one we use here) is an "ABCD" system. By this method, the top 20% of accounts within a territory receive an "A" classification. So if a sales territory has a total of 50 customers, the top 10 customers (based on expected profitability) would be classified as "A" accounts. The next 30% of the customers are "B" accounts, the following 30% are "C" accounts, and the final 20% are "D" customers.

Figure 14.5

Account Classification System

the top 20% of accounts, based on expected profits	**A** ACCOUNTS	the highest-priority accounts receive the highest percentage of your selling time
the second 30% of accounts	**B** ACCOUNTS	the next most important group of accounts receive the next biggest percentage of time dedication
the next 30% of accounts	**C** ACCOUNTS	these accounts are important but receive a lower priority (and percentage of selling time) than *A & B* accounts
the bottom 20% of accounts, based on profits	**D** ACCOUNTS	the least important group of accounts, receiving little or no selling time

The four-letter account classification system above is based on expected profitability. When listed in order of expected profits, the top 20% of accounts become A accounts. The subsequent 30% are classified as B accounts. The next 30% are C accounts. And the final 20% are D accounts. Priorities and selling time are allocated accordingly, with A accounts receiving the most and D accounts the least. Individual organizations may utilize a different classification system (one with only three letters, or perhaps several more levels). Regardless of the system though, it is valuable for salespeople to employ one. There are only a finite number of selling hours available to representatives over the course of a year, and they would be wise to apportion them carefully in order to maximize their return on time invested (R.O.T.I.).

Your organization may subscribe to a different classification system
— which is fine. The important thing is that your accounts are classified, and that your selling time is apportioned accordingly. But how do
we decide how much time each classification receives?

ALLOCATING YOUR SELLING TIME

How you allocate your selling time is ultimately driven by profitability.
Recall from the previous chapter that as part of the territory planning
process you need to determine what percentage of your time you plan
to dedicate to business creation, current account management, administrative, and/or other activities. Once you have made this determina-
tion, you will have a finite number of hours available to allocate to your
existing customers. It is based on the expected return customers will
bring that you classify accounts and allocate your selling time.

First, let's determine what percentage of your total expected territory profits you can expect from each type of account: total the expected profitability for each classification based on individual forecasts; then
divide this sum by the total expected profitability for the territory; multiply each result by 100 to determine the percentage of total expected
profits each classification represents.

Then, it's a simple matter of allocating your current account-management time to each of the classifications. For example, let's say that you
estimate 1,200 hours per year will be dedicated to your current customer
base and that the chart below represents the details of your territory.

ACCOUNT CLASSIFICATION	FORECASTED % OF TOTAL PROFITS	HOURS ALLOCATED OF 1200 AVAILABLE	NUMBER OF CUSTOMERS	ANNUAL HOURS PER CUSTOMER
A	45%	540	20	27
B	25%	300	30	10
C	20%	240	30	8
D	10%	120	20	6
Totals	100%	1200	100	--

Of course, this example of selling time allocation is only that —
an *example*. Some territories (based on factors such as geography,
industry, and distribution channels) may be drastically different from
the one examined. The important point to remember is that regard-

less of the territory or industry, it is valuable to go through this time allocation process in order to ensure R.O.T.I. is maximized.

As we have seen, local analysis (the second step of the account-management process) involves a complex series of activities activities. These are summarized in the "Personal Check" box at right.

The next step of the account-management process involves designing a critical path for each of your customers — a detailed action plan for realizing the expected value forecasted.

■**3** Critical path development

Designing a critical path requires that you specify a series of specific steps to be taken — along with an expected date of completion for each — in order to achieve account goals and targets. A critical path is the actual strategy you employ to maximize revenue within an account relationship.

First, assemble the results of your local analysis. Then consider the available information and outline all of the steps required to achieve your forecasts and goals. Include the date you plan to complete each step. Here are some other key issues to consider:

- **Break down quarterly targets** into monthly, weekly, and daily targets, and outline the steps required to reach each one.
- **Include every activity associated with the account**, including simple telephone calls, research, or preparation activities.
- **Use the time allocation** determined by your local analysis for the account; manage your R.O.T.I. effectively.
- **Determine which activities will yield the most profit** and plan accordingly.
- **Use various methods of contact.** For example, use the phone where it will be a more efficient use of your time. It's not always necessary to visit the client personally.
- **Write everything down.** It's advantageous to keep detailed lists and copies of the critical path handy at all times.

☑ *Personal Check*

Procedures for local analysis

☐ Assemble all available information on the account.

☐ Consider your global analysis (in your territory plan) as it relates directly to the account.

☐ Analyze the various buying influences at the account and identify problems areas or concerns (place warning signs where appropriate).

☐ Find at least one "coach."

☐ Complete the "What Am I Gonna Do At This Account?" analysis.

☐ Conduct a profitability forecast.

☐ Classify the account once forecasts have been completed.

☐ Determine how many hours are available for growth-oriented maintenance activities (current account management) based on account classification.

- **Where possible, attach all support documentation** to the critical path for future reference (for example, the analysis of the buying influences involved, the *"What Am I Gonna Do At This Account?"* analysis, the account forecast calculations, etc.).
- **Transfer each entry from the critical path to your appointment book.** (Recall from Chapter 9 the importance of using a closed-loop system to ensure things don't fall through the cracks. This will help you to ensure that each and every action step in the critical path is carried out by the expected completion date.)

To design effective critical paths, try using a model similar to the one shown on page 169. This is particularly useful, since it forces you to establish a list of time-bound action steps that you intend to take in order to achieve specific goals at a given account. You are also asked to outline the specific goals and targets you have set for the account. Remember to provide as much detail as possible on the critical path form; it may serve as your primary source of reference in your growth-oriented maintenance efforts.

GROWTH-ORIENTED MAINTENANCE

If you're like many salespeople, you probably spend a portion of your time just keeping in touch with your existing accounts. These "feeler" calls are designed to make sure everyone is feeling good about the account relationship. But if our primary goal is (as we have stressed so far) to maximize profit, are such visits an inefficient use of selling time?

It could be argued that all selling activities should be focused towards achieving profitability growth. In other words, the goal of all current account management activities should be *growth-oriented maintenance —*

Leverage from Strength

To determine the steps required to reach account goals and forecasts, ask yourself: *"What are my greatest strengths in this account relationship?"* There are many tools available to help you generate creative ideas and plans, but asking yourself this question is one of the most powerful.

Write down your answer to the question, and use the resulting list of strengths to develop an action plan for achieving your goals. Plan to use these strengths to your advantage and develop a strategy to turn areas of weakness into opportunities for improvement.

Figure 14.6

The Critical Path Outline

CRITICAL PATH

COVERING THE PERIOD: _____ TO_____

TERRITORY: _____

SALES REPRESENTATIVE: _____

| CUSTOMER: | |
| GOALS: | |

To Do	To Be Completed By

This tool is designed to help representatives outline the specific, time-bound steps they plan to take in order to reach defined account goals and targets and maximize profitability.

employing a strategy to improve profits at each of your current accounts, where every sales call is geared towards this growth.

Still, in some cases, it may be appropriate to spend time solidifying customer relationships with "feeler" calls. And there may be occasions when you need to deal with minor problems or administrative issues — things that aren't directly focused on growth-oriented maintenance.

So which is it? Are feeler calls a viable expenditure of selling time or not? The answer is: *"It depends"* — on your territory, your customer base, your industry, and your organization. In the end, there is a viable argument for adopting a strategy where you at least consider how to improve profitability at your accounts before, during, and after each sales call. Remember, one of your mandates is to maximize territory profitability — in the long and short term. So you should probably focus on growth-oriented maintenance whenever possible.

▬4 Act

The final step in the account management process is to *act* — or *implement your critical path*. Refer to your outline periodically to ensure that you are on track, then make adjustments as required. Most importantly, remember that account management is a dynamic, cyclical process. Once you have completed the items on your critical path or if there is a significant change in the situation at the account, begin the process again by taking a new snapshot.

Remember to use your time-management skills to prevent things from falling through the cracks. Your closed-loop system will help you ensure that you follow the steps of each critical path, reach the goals and forecasts for each account, and maximize territory profitability.

CYCLE TIME

Your relationships with customers, as well as the circumstances at each account, can change on a daily basis. Therefore, effective account goals, objectives, and critical paths must be continually refined.

The account-management process is designed to cover a specific period of time. The critical paths you establish for your accounts outline the steps you plan to take in order to accomplish a specific goal by a specific date. Therefore, even if everything goes according to your plan, the process begins again once the goal has been attained.

In our earlier examination of *territory planning*, we discussed the fact that the overall territory plan should ideally span a period of one business quarter. We also pointed out that *account planning* should be conducted even more often (although in tandem with territory planning).

Does your organization have a standard period of frequency for account planning? Does that standard correspond to what you've learned here? Regardless of the answers to these questions, consider the unique nature of your sales territory, your company, and your industry. Make an appointment with your manager to discuss the issue of territory and account planning frequency. Determine what period of time your overall territory plan and account critical paths should cover.

Principles of Account Management

Maximizing territory and account profitability is not a simple task. Indeed, it is actually quite complex. So take the time to review this chapter carefully. To help you here's a list of basic rules.

- Account management is a "living," dynamic process; use the four-step account-management process to help you manage it.

- Maximize profitability at each account; make sure all of your activities are geared towards this mission — and even if you make "feeler" calls, at least remember to consider how you can improve returns at the account before, during, and/or after the call.

- When conducting your local analysis for each account, be sure to consider all of the factors that could affect account profitability — including those identified during the global analysis — and the development of your strategic territory plan.

- Be sure you identify and manage all of the buying influences within a customer organization; and make sure you identify and meet the true economic buyer.

- You must have at least one "coach" for every account.

- Evaluate previous results and measure the actual payback of your activities, then modify account goals accordingly for the next period.

- Use the formula $PP + PG - RE = EV$ to forecast the expected profit from each account over a given period; pay special attention to PG (estimated gross profit growth), as it can be quite complex. Be sure to consider all of the factors.

- Classify your accounts, and allocate your selling time accordingly. Remember, there's not enough time available to dedicate an equal amount to all of your customers. Base your time allocation on your ability to maximize profitability (R.O.T.I.).

- Develop a detailed, time-bound critical path for each account.

- Account management is a cyclical process—it never stops.

SUMMARY

In this chapter we conducted a detailed examination of *the account-management process*. The specific steps of this process are listed below:

1. **The snapshot.** Assemble all of the available data on the account.

2. **Local analysis.** Re-examine the results of your global analysis (the *strategic territory plan*), and consider the strengths, weaknesses, opportunities, and threats you face at the account, on three levels (the competition, the marketplace, and your organization itself).

   • Analyze the buying influences within the organization.
   • Calculate the expected value of the account through the forecasting process.
   • Classify the account based on its expected value.
   • Allocate selling time to the account based on its classification.

3. **Critical path development**

   • Focus on growth-oriented maintenance activities.
   • Identify and capitalize on your points of greatest strength — use your leverage.

4. **Act**

   • Remember that account management is dynamic and cyclical. Therefore, the process must be conducted often.

Business Creation

So far in this book, we have looked at a number of skills and methods that you can use to achieve maximum profitability in your sales territory. Many of these techniques have focused on improving efficiency — that is, managing existing accounts to ensure the greatest possible return. Now it's time to look at another way to improve profitability — by securing new customers. This area of activity is known as *business creation*.

In today's competitive marketplace, successful salespeople need to be sophisticated in their business creation efforts. Gone are the days when door-to-door cold calls were the sole means of business creation. Sales professionals engage in networking, marketing, prospecting, and trade show activities (to name only a few) in their efforts to secure new customers and generate profitable sales growth.

Business creation has evolved into a multi-staged process of cultivating new clientele. It starts when you prepare for this cultivation process, building the target market from which you can draw prospective customers — a kind of "tilling the soil," you might say. Then the cultivation process gets under way. You initiate the process by moving potential customers from being part of the general target market to becoming genuine, qualified prospects. Next, you "grow" them to become one of the "hot" accounts that is ready to close a sale with you and your organization. The final step involves moving them forward to a favourable buying decision until, at the end, they become one of your new customers.

In this chapter we'll take a detailed look at this process, and how you can use it to build even greater sales and profits.

THE PROSPECTING FUNNEL

For many salespeople, a prospect is defined as anyone who isn't a customer. But this perspective is rather short-sighted. The fact is that a genuine prospect must have a need for (or at least an interest in) your product or service. And that's bound to place some limits on your list of prospects.

This is where the *prospecting funnel* comes in. It is a model that looks at all prospecting activities and forces you to ask the question: *"Is my time allocated properly in order to maintain a consistent flow of profit?"*

Organizations move through various stages in the transition from identified target to new client. The prospecting funnel is a tool that helps you take organizations through those stages. It's important to talk about this concept before we move on to the other aspects of business creation, because it provides a context for our discussions.

As you can see in Figure 15.1, opposite, the prospecting funnel consists of four transitional stages. First, you identify a *target market* within the global marketplace and sift through it to find organizations that *may* have a need or interest in your products or services (suspect accounts). Then, you employ *qualifying skills* to identify customers with a genuine need or interest (prospective accounts). The next transition involves actively nurturing prospective accounts towards becoming one of your *"hot ones."* And finally, hot prospects become new customers through further selling efforts.

In the following pages, we'll examine methods for moving organizations through each transition. But first, let's take a look at the characteristics of organizations at each stage of the prospecting funnel.

THE MARKETPLACE

This stage refers to the global marketplace as a whole — all countries, all industries, all organizations — and is located "above" the funnel. In most cases, of course, this marketplace is too broad a starting point for your business creation efforts. Therefore, the goal here is to narrow the market quickly and identify *suspects*.

SUSPECT ACCOUNTS

Suspect accounts are those that *may* have a need or interest in your product or service.(They are at the top level of the funnel.) Statistically, these are the accounts that may result in an order. They are described as

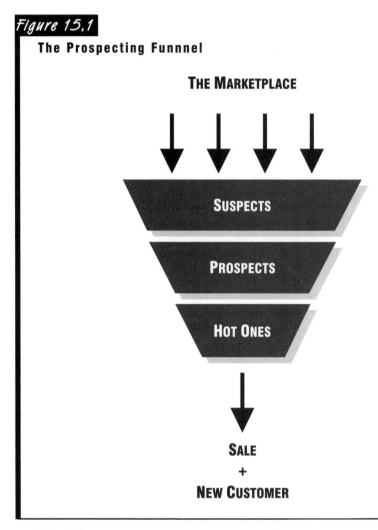

Figure 15.1

The Prospecting Funnnel

This model illustrates the various stages of the prospecting process. Suspect accounts are found in the target market and show a possible interest in your products/services. By nurturing suspects using your qualifying skills you are able to turn customers into genuine *prospects*. From here, it is a matter of further nurturing to bring accounts to the stage where they are ready to order and appear fully committed to you and your organization—these are your *"hot ones."* Finally, through further development you are able to reach agreement with your hot prospects, converting them to new clients. This model was adapted from The Sales Funnel discussed in Robert B. Miller & Stephen E. Heiman's book *Strategic Selling*[SM], ©1985.

leads which, traditionally, have been actively sought out by sales representatives. Even so, their viability as genuine customers is unconfirmed. The goal with suspect accounts is to qualify them in order to turn them into *prospects*.

PROSPECT ACCOUNTS

Prospects are those accounts where identified needs or interests exist. They are found at the middle level of the funnel. With these accounts you have identified *at least* one buying influence and research verifies the possibility that an order will result. The important thing to do with prospects is "cover the bases." Your goal is to create and implement account plans in order to define further selling opportunities and gain the support of all buying influences.

"HOT ONES"

Through effective account management, selected prospect accounts will become "hot ones." These are accounts where an order is expected in half (or less) of the normal selling cycle. All buying influences have been contacted and support your proposition. The next steps should be clear to you in order to bring a deal to completion — there should be little or no luck involved. You should have no warning signs left concerning any of the buying influences. Your goal here is to close the sale.

So, now that we understand what the situation looks like at each stage of the funnel, the real work comes in understanding how to move accounts through the various transitions.

FROM MARKET TO SUSPECT

The first transition in the prospecting funnel — from global market to identified suspect — is often the most arduous. (At this point, we are still above the funnel.) There are three large steps involved in this transition, as outlined below.

◀1 Identifying your target market

The global marketplace is huge, comprising a vast number of industries and organizations throughout the world. Identifying which ones you intend to target with your selling efforts is the first step in turning accounts into suspects.

Often, this effort is undertaken by senior executives as part of organizational planning. But just as often, it is left up to you. In either case, you should thoroughly understand the specifics of your intended target market.

As you might expect, there are many variables to consider when defining your target market. Some of the principal variables include:

- industry type;
- organization size;
- specific organizational needs or interests;
- customer distribution channels;
- the competition; and
- you, your products, services, and organization.

◀2 Identifying tools and sources of leads

During the market-to-suspect phase, you use many tools to identify potential suspect accounts. (Several of these tools are discussed in detail in Chapter 17: Marketing and Promotion.) The main purpose here is to list the possible sources or tools available to you. These include:

- intuition;
- rumours;
- tips;
- referrals;
- networking;
- direct-mail campaigns;
- trade shows;
- corporate marketing initiatives;
- multi-media marketing;
- telemarketing programs;
- advertising;
- trade journals and magazines;
- directories;
- existing customer lists;
- lost business;
- professional data bases; and
- trade associations;

◀3 Identify suspects

Our focus here is to use the list of sources or tools to create a list of suspect accounts. This is accomplished by generating a series of criteria to identify suspect accounts from each source or tool. For example, you might identify the manufacturing sector as having a significantly greater interest or need for your product than other industry sectors. So this would become one of the criteria for identifying suspect accounts.

Once you have identified all your criteria, use your sources and tools to select organizations that meet those criteria. Generate a comprehensive list of these organizations. This list will become your master *suspect list*. From this you may wish to generate more focused lists — for a specific source, perhaps, or a region. Regardless, you'll want to maintain a master list of your suspect accounts.

It is important to keep the accounts that appear on your suspect list to a reasonable number: too many and it will become unmanageable; too few and you won't have enough to work with as you move further down the prospecting funnel.

FROM SUSPECT TO PROSPECT

We are now at the top level of the funnel. Here, in order to turn suspect accounts into prospect accounts, you need to employ your qualifying skills.

Prospect accounts are those where you have verified a need or interest in your product. The only way to accomplish this is to contact one of the buying influences. Therefore, in order for an account to progress from suspect to prospect, at least one buying influence must be contacted — and preferably more. Remember, the more thoroughly you qualify client needs and interests, the better your chances for success as you progress further down the funnel.

Regardless of how well you identify qualified suspects, keep in mind that a large percentage of them may never become prospects. It is often said that if you can maintain a 20% closure rate (the percentage of suspect accounts that ultimately become new customers) then you should consider yourself lucky. And it is here, in the suspect-to-prospect transition, that much of the remaining 80% will fall out of the prospecting funnel. This can be the most frustrating and demoralizing aspect of business creation, and often leads to "prospecting procrastination" — a condition where salespeople fail to contact suspect accounts because they want to avoid the demoralizing effect of rejection.

How can you keep from falling into the vortex of "prospecting procrastination"? Think of prospecting simply as an activity where you identify organizations that you are able to help. If suspect accounts decline your proposition, they are not saying "no" to you as a person; they are only saying that your product is not what they need or want right now. Viewed from this perspective, you'll be able to deal with rejection, while reducing its potentially debilitating psychological effects.

Contacting suspects directly is an effective way of promoting them to genuine prospects. Once you've contacted an account, you should meet with at least one buying influence to gather valuable information. By using your question-asking skills (recall our discussion of this subject in Chapter 4), you will be able to uncover the information required to determine customer needs and interests.

If you are able to verify genuine need or interest, the suspect account becomes qualified as a *prospect account*. If not, you should consider one of two possibilities. The first is that you misqualified the suspect account; they really don't have any need for (or interest in) your product, nor are they likely to in the future. In this case, the suspect account is relegated back to the wider global marketplace. The second possibility is that the suspect account fails to qualify *now* but may in the future. In this case, the account is removed from the funnel, but remains a viable candidate within your target market.

Keep detailed notes on every suspect account you contact. They may be useful when the account becomes a prospect. And if the account falls out of the funnel but remains in your target market, you will have the notes to refer to at a later date. Be sure to record a follow-up date with these accounts to verify any changes in their status — they may become a suspect again in the future.

Maintain a master list of all your active prospects. Once you have promoted an account to prospect status, add it to the list, keeping in mind what we said earlier about managing the number of accounts: if you have too many prospect accounts, the list becomes unmanageable; too few, and new business growth cannot be sustained.

From prospect to "hot one"

We are now in the heart of the funnel, where genuine prospects are nurtured to become the much-cherished "hot ones."

Here you'll need well developed strategic skills — particularly your account management skills. The reason is that prospective customers are treated much the same way as existing ones. The challenge is to cultivate the prospect relationship carefully and "cover all the bases" (as discussed in the previous chapter).

Given that you have already verified the prospect's needs or interests (otherwise the prospect wouldn't be a prospect), the next step is to gain the customer's commitment to establishing a supplier relationship with you. There are several steps in this process.

1 Conduct research

The first step in moving from prospect to "hot one" is to gather as much information as possible concerning the account. Typical information-gathering activities are listed below.

- Gather general information on the organization, products, services, and industry.
- Assemble strategic information on the prospect's situation by
  - contacting trade associations, chambers of commerce, government and public libraries, and databases;
  - assessing the current financial condition of the organization; and
  - analyzing current supplier relationships (for example, who they are buying from, what they are buying).
- Determine and analyze the various buying influences involved.
- Assess internal business systems and processes: where possible, observe the prospective organization in its main business function.
- Speak to others who deal with the organization and the various buying influences.

2 Consider strategic issues

There are two principal strategic issues to keep in mind during the prospect-to-"hot one" phase.

- Ensure that you reach all of the various buying influences involved (as outlined in the previous chapter).

- Position yourself to make optimal use of your benefit selling, value-added selling, and presentation skills. In other words, the goal is to get each buying influence to agree on the genuine *benefits* of your proposition and how that proposition differentiates you from the competition.

⬛ 3 Use research to implement strategies

In order to move an account from a prospect to one of your "hot ones," you need to use the information gathered during your research activities to accomplish the following tasks.

- Further qualify the organization's need and interest in your products or services — verify the *appropriateness* of your role as the supplier.
- Identify the core benefits that you can offer the customer. Outline how you plan to demonstrate them to each of the buying influences. Prepare strong, compelling statements. Use influential, penetrating questions. (Recall our discussion of open probes, closed probes, and high-gain questions in Chapter 4.)
- Assess the various selling opportunities that exist within the organization and assign priorities to them.

Profit Priorities

Be sure to assess the potential profitability of each prospect in order to give it the appropriate priority. As with current account management, there is only a finite amount of time available for business creation activities. In order to maximize profitability, you need to set priorities for your opportunities and allocate your time accordingly.

Recall from earlier chapters that you can calculate the estimated value of any prospective account with the basic formula outlined below.

$$EP - RE = EV$$

or

Expected Profits (EP) − Required Expenses (RE) = Estimated Value (EV)

Arrange prospective accounts in priority based on their expected value, and then apportion a specific amount of time in order to maximize R.O.T.I. This data can then be incorporated into the critical path for each prospective account. By allocating available hours effectively, you can improve your efforts to reach established goals for the prospect.

- Set primary and secondary goals.
- Devise a critical path of time-bound action steps to achieve defined goals.
- Ensure that you have:
  - mastered the required product knowledge;
  - identified and organized all required materials and data; and
  - prepared yourself to deal with expected customer objections.
- Provide value-added service by *exceeding* the expectations of each buying influence.
- Contact each buying influence and gain commitment for your proposal. This could involve multiple meetings, presentations, and telephone calls.
- Revise your critical path constantly in order to achieve your goals in the prescribed time frames.

4 Manage prospect conversion

The rate of conversion from prospect to "hot one" is generally much higher than that from suspect to prospect. In fact, as a potential customer moves down the funnel, your chances of further progress increase substantially.

However, conversion during this transition is rarely 100%. For example, you may not be able to move the prospect down the funnel because of a lack of information or a problem with one of the buying influences. In this case, continue to plan and work the account carefully.

(As noted in the "Profit Priorities" box on the previous page, remember to manage the amount of time you spend on the account so that your R.O.T.I. is acceptable; it's often tempting to spend too much time on an account simply because we want to see it move forward.)

Another obstacle to conversion may be that the prospect's original impetus has changed — the prospect may have a new business plan or decided to go in an entirely different direction. In this case, determine if the account is still a viable prospect (perhaps for a different product or service, or in a different area of the customer organization), or if it has now reverted back to suspect status, or if the account is no longer viable at all, in which case it returns to the global market.

Unfortunately, there will also be some instances where the account has decided to work with one of your competitors on the project. Here, the customer's needs may be totally satisfied by the competitor or there may still be some needs that remain unfulfilled — it depends upon the product or service in question. For example, the need for the "big-ticket" items may have been filled, but not the need for related consumables. In another instance, the prospect may have signed a purchasing agreement for only a specific period of time. Ultimately, in situations where the prospect has chosen the competition, it is your responsibility to determine the new status of the account — and to develop a new strategy for that account. You can then proceed to manage the account as a prospect, as a suspect, as part of the target market, or you can consign it back to the global market. So, depending on the circumstances, a prospect that does not progress down the funnel to become a "hot one" may fall out of the funnel, move backwards up the funnel, or stay exactly where it is.

Whatever action you take, remember to keep your notes up to date for each prospect file. This way you have an automatic reference for any information you may require. Also, be sure to record in your appointment book all activities from prospect critical paths. This will prevent things from falling through the cracks. Common practice dictates that you should participate in some form of business creation activity each day.

From "hot one" to customer

The final transition in the business creation process may actually be the easiest. We are now out the bottom of the funnel.

Once prospects acquire the status of "hot ones," chances are that you will have contacted all of the buying influences, and they are supportive of your proposal. All that remains is a formal agreement. Reaching this stage should require only administrative, process-oriented tasks, where there is little opportunity to cancel or stall the project.

You should reach a formal agreement in half (or less) of the normal selling cycle. You should be absolutely clear as to what must be done to bring the project to a favourable completion.

You can rely upon your relationship with the various buying influences, along with your closing and negotiation skills, to bring the project to completion as soon as possible. The key to success during this transition is to remain customer-oriented, exceeding the expectations of each buying influence and, at the same time, remain focused on taking the steps required to complete the sale. Remember, *you must ask for the order or commitment* — don't procrastinate.

The conversion rate on "hot ones" to new customers is typically very high. Rarely does an account fall out of the funnel or stall at this point. If an account is a genuine "hot one," then all of the buying influences are in favour of you and your products or services. Therefore, there is very little that can go wrong.

Cases in which a "hot one" does not convert to a new customer are usually the result of a salesperson misjudging when to move them down the funnel. For example, he or she may not have secured the full support of all buying influences, or there may have been other obstacles to overcome that were not uncovered. Ultimately, it is only the salesperson who can determine if the account should fall out of the funnel, move backwards up the funnel, or stay exactly where it is. Based on that decision, you can generate effective strategic plans.

You will benefit from continuing to plan and develop critical paths for "hot ones," ensuring that all details are anticipated. Remember to record all activities in your appointment book to prevent things from being forgotten. Make detailed notes in each customer file, providing an automatic record for reference purposes, as required.

Again, it is unwise to keep too many accounts on your "hot ones" list. You should expect that once an account becomes a "hot one," the transition to new-customer status is forthcoming. In this way, you ensure optimal flow through the funnel, thereby enhancing your business creation efforts.

MANAGING FUNNEL FLOW

Throughout this chapter we have discussed the importance of managing the number of accounts you have at each stage of the funnel. One of the keys to effective business creation is to control the flow of accounts down the funnel at all times.

As a rule, you should maintain *many* suspects, *several* prospects, and a *select few* "hot ones." This type of proportion is essential to maintaining a consistent revenue flow from new customers. And a consistent flow of

Keeping Your Customer a Customer

One of the keys to sales success is *constantly exceed customer expectations.* Consider the times when you've had a very good experience in a retail store — so good that you want to return and would recommend the store to anyone. Chances are you enjoyed the experience because your expectations as a customer were exceeded. The same principle can be applied in business-to-business and industrial sales situations.

Given this premise, it only makes sense to establish formal customer-service standards, procedures, and programs — and to embrace them enthusiastically. These are elements of what we call *the customer care process.* Here are some important issues to consider when developing customer care standards, procedures, and programs.

- Identify the critical components of effective customer care programs and processes — identify what your customers' expectations are and how you can establish programs to exceed those expectations continuously.
- Identify the best practices of your customers' other suppliers.
- Create and maintain comprehensive, up-to-date customer records, covering all account and business information, including:
  - personal data on buying influences, their likes and dislikes;
  - customer expectations regarding products and services;
  - the customer's desired method and frequency of contact;
  - what the customer considers to be value-added; and
  - how the customer prefers to provide you with feedback.
- Classify customers (as A, B, C, or D) and tailor your standards, processes, and programs to meet the needs of each classification ("A" customers may not have the same expectations as "C" customers).
- Modify existing processes and programs to accommodate newly defined customer service standards.
- Create additional strategies for exceeding the needs and expectations of customers, as required — especially "A" customers; remember, they may represent up to 50% of your entire territory revenue.

If your customer care programs and processes embrace these considerations, it will help you cement long-standing, mutually beneficial relationships with your accounts.

Figure 15.2

Prospecting Funnel Summary

SUSPECTS	PROSPECTS	HOT ONES

A summary chart similar to this one can be used to manage all business creation activities. At any one time, the chart can be completed to create a snapshot of the current business creation situation. In this way, representatives can determine which aspects of The Prospecting Funnel require their attention and, therefore, allocate time accordingly.

new revenue is critical to achieving maximum profitability in your business-creation efforts.

For example, let's say that you have many "hot ones," few prospects, and many suspects. Chances are you will eventually run out of "hot ones" (once they become customers, there will be few prospects to progress down the funnel), which may lead to a "dry period" in new business generation. Such variations in business volume rarely help in achieving maximum profitability — which is why each stage of the funnel requires active management.

Every salesperson understands the importance of searching for new accounts to add to the funnel. But accounts should not be added until the timing is right. In fact, you can benefit from "working" the funnel backwards. As organizations fall through the funnel to become new customers, prospects can be promoted to "hot ones." And as prospects move down the funnel, suspects can be promoted to fill the gap. Finally, as suspects become prospects, new suspects can be identified to replace them.

The number of accounts that should be maintained at each stage depends on the individual salesperson, the organization, and the industry. A primary determining factor is the percentage of available working hours that will be dedicated to business-creation activities.

As you may recall from our discussion of territory planning in

Chapter 13, the more hours you dedicate to business creation, the more accounts you can manage at each stage. In any case, however, you should rarely have more than a handful of genuine "hot ones."

The prospecting funnel can be widely applied to managing all of your business-creation activities. With a summary chart (see figure 15.2, previous page), you can classify potential customers according to their respective progress through the funnel, and thereby determine how to invest your available business-creation time. If the funnel is in equilibrium, you can focus your efforts on converting "hot ones" to new customers. If the number of "hot ones" is low, then perhaps you should focus on nurturing prospects. If the number of prospects is low, then maybe qualifying suspects is the main concern. And finally, if the number of suspects is low, you may need to sift through the target market to identify legitimate additions.

As we have seen, the prospecting funnel is a valuable tool for sales professionals, enabling them to maximize business creation efficiencies. This, in turn, allows representatives to achieve a consistent flow of new business revenues, leading to maximized territory profitability.

SUMMARY

1. Business creation is an important component of most sales professionals' jobs. In order to maximize territory profitability, you need to secure new customers and pursue business opportunities. The *prospecting funnel* is a tool that helps representatives manage these efforts.

2. The process of identifying new customers starts with the *global marketplace*. This may be narrowed down — by industry type, for example — to determine the *target market*. Where an account appears to have a possible need for, or interest in, your product, it becomes a *suspect*.

3. You use qualifying skills to verify that the account has a possible need for, or interest in, the products or services being offered, and that there is a reasonable expectation of an eventual order. The account is now a *prospect*.

4. By applying sophisticated tactical selling skills, your next step is to gain the support of all buying influences involved and prepare to close the deal. Once accomplished, this elevates the status of the account to *"hot one."*

5. The final transition through the funnel is quite simple. By following a detailed critical path to ensure that nothing falls through the cracks, you complete all of the administrative and other requirements involved. Then, through persistence and perseverance — and *by asking for the order* (perhaps several times) — the deal is done.

6. By doing what it takes to maintain a consistent flow of accounts from one stage of the funnel to the next, you can enhance your ability to secure new business opportunities and maximize territory profitability.

Administration and Reporting

For most sales professionals, administrative and reporting duties make up at least part of their job responsibilities. Here we examine the importance of these duties and discuss some specific tasks in detail.

Although this chapter is relatively short, the subject matter is nevertheless important. Administration and reporting may appear to be merely subsidiary tasks, yet they are essential to your ability to maximize profitability.

INFORMATION IS AN ASSET

In the course of your day-to-day activities, you create a substantial amount of data — through sales reports, expense reports, call reports, and other paperwork. This data is a highly valuable resource for salespeople and management. Once processed, it becomes useful *information*. And in a world that increasingly equates knowledge with power, this information is a critical asset to sales success.

When you have the information you need, you and your organization are better positioned to stay ahead of the competition and remain successful. Information allows you to develop strategies and plans. It enables you to make subtle shifts in tactics and processes. It enables you to strive for continuous improvement.

Administration and reporting activities create the data that provides important feedback to management. As a salesperson, *you* are the one who knows what is happening in your portion of the marketplace. *You* are the one who can see which ideas are working, which ones aren't, and what it is that customers want. In fact, chances are that you and your administration and reporting efforts are the only real information conduit available to management. In a larger sense, the information gathered through these means may be critical to the success of the organization. Senior management steers the organization and develops overall business plans and strategies — something that can't be done effectively without the information that you provide. So the apparently mundane tasks of administration and reporting are actually critical to overall organizational success.

Conversely, the data that allows management to generate effective business plans and strategies also benefits you. It allows management to provide you and your peers with more direction, better tools, enhanced resources, and enlightened leadership. Moreover, the data gathered through sales administration and reporting can help you refine your efforts to maximize territory profitability. It provides you with an instant snapshot of your territory at any given time. And this information serves as a wonderful benchmark for comparison on territory (or even individual account) performance.

Here are some specific examples of the sales administration and reporting function:

- Share relevant customer feedback internally with other members of the team, including sales management.
- Report on specific sales situations for strategic purposes, allowing you to build additional sales approaches and strategies.
- Share specific product ideas, market opportunities, and customer satisfaction levels with various internal departments.
- Build rapport with customers and suppliers — thus generating new business opportunities — by sharing non-privileged information (such as market statistics or customer satisfaction information).
- Provide value-added services and advice to customers by identifying buying patterns, leading to possible savings through volume discounting or inventory management interventions.

ADMINISTRATION AND REPORTING METHODS

Organizations and industries differ. Some sales professionals have very demanding administration and reporting duties; others have virtually none. Determining factors may include: the size and sophistication of the organization; the competitive nature of the industry or marketplace; the management style employed internally; and the products and ser-

Using Available Information

The data gathered from sales administration and reporting is valuable not only to management's planning activities, but to your sales efforts, as well. When this data is compiled and comes back to you in the form of a report or information bulletin, be sure to take advantage of it. Here are some specific recommendations.

- Set aside time to read sales information and reports.
- Read and understand management information (company reports, strategic goals, corporate mission or vision statements, marketing and business plans, and so on).
- Use available data to revise your territory plan, sales forecasts, account plans, and critical paths.
- Share valuable (non-privileged) information with customers regarding buying/product-usage history and performance.
- Familiarize yourself with all new product information as it becomes available.

vices involved. There is no "best" system. It is up to salespeople and management to work together to determine the ideal system for their organization.

Reports and paperwork

There is a wide variety of reports and paperwork that salespeople are typically required to complete. Let's look at some of the main types.

CALL REPORTS

These reports provide the details of your sales activities, including: number of sales calls made; customers visited; business-creation activities conducted; new customers secured; customers lost; sales volume and profitability for the period; returned products and orders; type of activities conducted with existing customers; and product demonstrations conducted.

CUSTOMER PROFILES

Many organizations keep a comprehensive profile of each customer, including name, address, information about various buying influences, buying history and product usage, as well as a diary of all contacts with the customer. It is often the salesperson's responsibility to complete new profiles, if not maintain them. Profiles should be updated regularly with all information relating to the customer. In many cases, the account plan and critical path for each customer are kept together with the profile.

CREDIT APPLICATIONS

When you have secured a new customer and credit terms are part of that relationship, then you may need to receive credit approval before the account can be established. In these cases, you could be responsible for completing the application and forwarding it to the appropriate personnel within your organization.

ORDER FORMS OR REQUISITIONS

In many organizations, an order form or requisition is required in order to effect a customer sale. You may be called upon to complete these forms as part of the final step in the sales process.

PROPOSALS

The selling process often requires you to submit a formal (or informal) written proposal or quotation to a customer. This document typically contains all of the relevant details of the sales contract, including the price, the products or services to be provided, the terms of sale, delivery details, and product specifications.

SALES FORECASTS AND BUDGETS

As we've seen in previous chapters, one of your most important responsibilities as a salesperson is to forecast the expected value of prospective and current customers. In some cases, these forecasts must be submitted formally to sales management.

TERRITORY AND ACCOUNT PLANS

Similarly, you must also generate overall territory and individual account plans, along with specific critical paths — again, often as formal submissions to management.

EXPENSE REPORTS

Salespeople are usually reimbursed for expenses they incur in their efforts to manage a sales territory. As part of this process, an employer may require you to provide an accounting or record of the expenses incurred. In many organizations, a salesperson must complete expense reports on a monthly or weekly basis.

Regardless of the administrative and reporting systems employed within your organization, the important thing is to keep up with the necessary paperwork and submit it on time. In many cases, it can have an impact on the transaction between you and the customer; in others, it may determine whether you (and your management) have the information needed.

Administration activities

In addition to reports and paperwork, you may also be required to perform a variety of other administrative duties. For example, you may have service or merchandising responsibilities as well as sales responsibilities. Regardless of your job description, you probably have more administrative duties than we've discussed so far.

Some of the other administrative activities that you may be responsible for are outlined below.

- setting up new customer accounts in the organization's computer system;
- completing order entry in an on-line computer system;
- checking inventory levels in order to schedule shipments and inform customers of availability;
- coordinating interdepartmental functions and processes;
- coordinating outside resources;
- conducting interdepartmental meetings;
- keeping in touch with clients regarding the status of orders, shipments, or invoices;
- collecting accounts receivable;
- customizing work and orders when necessary;
- assuming responsibility for ensuring that work and orders are completed to the customer's satisfaction;
- Handling complaints and returns; and
- coordinating merchandising and marketing programs.

The important thing here is to conduct yourself as a professional at all times. Conduct yourself dutifully and complete tasks and responsibilities promptly. Ultimately, the effective performance of all duties — even the administrative ones — can contribute to overall territory profitability and success.

MISCELLANEOUS TASKS

Some other job responsibilities or tasks to keep in mind are those little things we often forget. These are the commonsense things that we sometimes take for granted, with the result that they often slip through the cracks. Don't let them!

Here are some of those "little" jobs to remember.

- gathering, organizing, and reviewing sales information wherever possible;
- reading or listening to to all memos, updates, faxes, messages, e-mail, voice mail, and files — company and customer alike — and responding promptly;
- keeping thorough customer records;
- maintaining all other data files (electronic or hard-copy) as required; and
- organizing and updating:
  - sample price lists;
  - brochures and product literature;
  - samples;
  - catalogues;
  - point of sale materials; and
  - other business tools, as required.

SUMMARY

1. As a salesperson, you will probably be responsible for many different administrative and reporting functions. These are important for your sales efforts and for management planning.

2. It is through upward organizational communication that critical information about customers' needs and interests, the industry, and the marketplace in general can be provided to senior management. Without this information, managers are essentially "blind."

3. Sales reports allow you to assess your current performance against your plans and objectives. In this way, you can adjust your course and make changes necessary for improvement.

4. Your focus on the value and importance of internal reporting and administration will position you to realize improved performance within your sales territory.

Marketing and Promotion

Over the past few decades — even the past few years — your role as a salesperson has changed significantly. Today, you must be an effective business manager as much as a sales representative. Your responsibilities are no longer restricted merely to making cold-calls and dealing with customers. Just as often you need to become involved in sales support activities such as marketing, telemarketing, advertising, networking, and merchandising. These are the activities we'll be examining in this chapter.

Marketing and promotional activities are generally designed to complement your business-creation efforts. They help to generate customer interest in you, your products and services, and your organization. They can help you define your target market, and identify suspect accounts (for your prospecting funnel). These functions qualify marketing and promotion as strategic (rather than tactical or self-management) activities. They are part of the planning efforts that you undertake "behind the scenes" in order to maximize territory profitability.

Since industries and organizations differ, there may be some specific aspects of marketing and promotion that are not discussed in this chapter. Our examination here covers some of the more common types of activity.

REGIONAL AND CORPORATE MARKETING

In our discussion of the planning pyramid (Chapter 13), you may recall that the sales plan is shown as the next level up from the marketing plan. In other words, sales and marketing have an *interdependent* relationship — they rely upon each other on a fundamental level. So it's not surprising that salespeople often become involved in regional and corporate marketing efforts.

DEVELOPING A PLAN

Typically, marketing and promotional activities begin with the development of a formal plan which examines the marketplace and outlines the various marketing or promotion efforts that can be employed to maximize business creation and overall profitability. These plans are often undertaken as part of the overall corporate marketing plan, although they may be part of a stand-alone regional or territory plan.

While the plans will differ for individual salespeople, organizations, and industries, most will attempt to accomplish the following:

- Establish a marketing and promotion budget.
- Refer to your territory and account goals, strategies, and plans.
- Outline specific goals and objectives for your marketing and promotion activities.
- Identify all possible marketing and promotion vehicles, such as advertising, direct mail, and telemarketing.
- Select the appropriate activities to reach your goals — those that:
  - fit the budget;
  - are linked to your sales strategies and action plans;
  - are appropriate for your target market and customer base;
  - exceed customers' expectations; and
  - will produce the desired results.

While corporate marketing plans are generally the responsibility of management, you can contribute to these plans by participating in focus group activities and providing market feedback. Remember, you may offer a uniquely valuable perspective on the marketplace and customer needs and interests.

Creating your own marketing initiatives

In many cases, it makes sense to develop your own marketing initiatives, even if they are not specified by regional or territory marketing plans. (Keep in mind, however, that such initiatives should complement those specified by the plans.) Here are some of the initiatives you can consider.

- Publish a regular customer newsletter.
- Publish a customer-specific manual.
- Personalize corporate ads to use within the territory at a local level.

- Reprint corporate newsletters or announcements with a personal introduction and distribute them to customers.
- Write an information column for a local newspaper or business publication (on topics relating to your business but geared to appeal to a broad reading audience).
- Contact local charities to develop programs.
- Sponsor local sporting events.

Researching the Market

What are your potential customers' likes, dislikes, needs, objectives, and interests? This is the kind of information typically acquired through market research. Such research can be comprehensive and formal (perhaps involving an outside market research firm), or informal and quite simple.

In organizations that conduct formal market research, salespeople are generally not involved in research activities (although they will probably make use of the research data). Even so, a salesperson is (or should be) always conducting market research on an informal basis. This is, as we discussed in the last chapter, part of the reporting function.

Effective salespeople are constantly asking questions. And some of those questions should attempt to gather information about the marketplace and about customers' needs, interests, and objectives.

Here are a few guidelines to consider when conducting your informal market research.

- Allocate time each week for informal research — perhaps making it part of every sales call.

- Conduct customer surveys on new products and services, overall satisfaction, the levels of customer service provided, etc.

- Conduct customer advisory councils.

- Coordinate small focus group sessions with customers to gain opinions on existing service or desired service enhancements.

- Monitor the performance of your various products and lines.

- When conducting market research activities, focus on the research — don't try to sell (customers will be less likely to share information).

- Be sure to publish your findings. Share the information with senior management, your customers, your prospects, and your suppliers.

IMPLEMENTING YOUR INITIATIVES

Once personalized marketing initiatives have been developed, there are a number of ways you can implement them. For example:

- Sell or distribute company display material, ad programs, or promotional material.
- Distribute mailings, faxes, and e-mail to branch offices.
- Get acquainted with editors of local magazines and newspapers.
- Work with the local print and broadcast media to gain exposure through interviews or phone-ins.

KEEPING IN TIME

While all the marketing efforts we've described may prove beneficial to business creation, remember to account for the time involved. Are these efforts part of your business creation activities, or are they accounted for separately? Depending on how you've decided to allocate your time in the territory planning process, some of these marketing and promotional activities will have to be done on your own time.

NETWORKING

One of the most common forms of marketing and promotion used today is networking — just look at the lunches, dinners, and other events that seem to pervade association and organization calendars. Typically, these gatherings present easy avenues for salespeople to meet with colleagues, competitors, clients, and prospective customers alike. They can provide ideal opportunities to learn, as well as improve marketplace awareness of you, your organization, and your products and services.

Where appropriate, it's generally a good idea to engage in networking activities at least once per month, if not more often.

Start by defining the market or industry segment that best captures your target market. Then identify those organizations, associations, and groups that represent your defined market segment. (Some possibilities are listed in the "Personal Check" box on this page.)

☑ *Personal Check*

Networking opportunities

- ❑ Chambers of commerce
- ❑ Local business councils
- ❑ Economic development groups
- ❑ Trade councils/associations
- ❑ Local business groups
- ❑ Professional organizations
- ❑ Local charity groups
- ❑ Boards of trade

As a member of your chosen group(s), your level of involvement will ultimately determine your networking success. Here are some suggestions for successful networking.

- Volunteer for active roles in the groups you join — participate in committees, or fill an executive position.
- Work the network; collect clues and information from members.
- Involve your key customers in relevant association events.
- Identify opportunities for association selling, such as benefit programs for memberships.
- Start breakfast clubs for reciprocally interested parties; here you should:
  - set objectives of programs;
  - coordinate meeting places;
  - arrange for guest speakers;
  - present information seminars; and
  - help customers get additional business.
- Build your profile in the industry; become a recognized expert in your field.
- Arrange events such as golf tournaments and baseball games for customers and colleagues.

DIRECT MAIL

From time to time, you may find it useful to conduct direct-mail campaigns. This may be as simple and informal as sending a flyer or brochure to your existing or prospective customers. On the other hand, you may become involved in large-scale, formal campaigns. In either case, you can use the following steps for just about any direct-mail activity.

1 Plan the campaign

- Establish your strategies.
- Identify the various centres of influence — by industry sector and geographic area.
- Build a database of suspect accounts.
- Segment the database by marketing sector.

- Create or identify direct mail materials, including:
  - sales materials;
  - target letters;
  - newsletters;
  - product reviews;
  - association or trend updates summaries;
  - corporate videos;
  - new product teasers; and
  - reminders for fill-in or repeat orders.
- Use effective business writing skills (refine your own or solicit assistance from a professional).
- Gain your organization's approval of the materials.

2 Generate your list of suspect accounts

- Use available professional publications (for example, Dun and Bradstreet reports, city or trade directories, and specialized industry journals.
- Purchase lists of leads from brokers.
- Input the suspect accounts into the database by industry sector.

3 Implement the campaign

- Arrange the actual delivery and timing of the material.
- Design a critical path for follow-up activities.
- Conduct comprehensive follow-up by mail, telephone, and in person.

4 Analyze the results

- Measure the campaign's return on investment, comparing new profits generated to the overall cost of the program.

5 Market national programs

- Use the applicable steps from your own program to implement national programs for your organization.

EDUCATION AND TRAINING

Customer education and training may be an important component of your marketing and promotion efforts. Why? Simply because an educated customer is generally a better customer.

Typically, areas of education and training will include:

- the use of machinery, equipment, or other products;
- the benefits of your product or service;
- how to sell your products to their customers;
- how to sell your sales proposition to their bosses;
- industry trends, shifts, and developments;
- government regulations regarding your products or services, or the industry itself; or
- how to train others on your products.

Customer training can be formal or informal, depending on the issues to be covered. For example, many of the items listed above can be covered during regularly scheduled sales meetings — you might discuss, say, industry developments during normal conversations or small-talk (if appropriate for that customer). If you are dealing with larger groups, however, it may be necessary to conduct more formal training programs.

Informal training sessions

Where training and education will be conducted informally, keep the following concepts in mind when planning for and conducting your session:

- Be empathetic.
- Don't be condescending to individuals — just because they don't know the things you do, it doesn't make you any better.
- Be humble — maybe you will learn something.
- Be sure to cover only information that is relevant to the customer.
- Go slowly, and make sure the customer understands before moving on.
- Be sure the customer sees the benefit to him/her of the issues being discussed.

◼ Formal training sessions

In situations where you will be conducting formal training programs, there are many factors to consider. For example, before embarking upon a large training project, you may wish to conduct independent research on training technologies, instructional design, adult learning principles, and training delivery. You might also consider preparing for the project by taking a "train-the-trainer" course.

Once you are adequately prepared to conduct formal customer training and education, consider the following steps.

1. PLAN YOUR EVENTS CAREFULLY

Some training initiatives you may wish to consider include:

- Create product seminars or training sessions (possibly in cooperation with affiliated suppliers).
- Organize public relations sessions with customers or sales associates.
- Arrange for guest speakers to talk at local schools.
- Take students on internships.
- Conduct local events such as "open houses" or plant tours.

2. ORGANIZE THE EVENT AND TRAINING MATERIALS

- Select an appropriate speaker for your audience.
- Create a "subject matter" document (if appropriate) as a promotional piece for the target audience.
- Create or source customer sales literature, such as product brochures, if required.
- Arrange event offerings and handouts for participants.
- Test your visual aids and materials.

3. ORGANIZE THE ADMINISTRATIVE DETAILS FOR THE EVENT

- Hire the people you'll need, such as contract staff or caterers.
- Arrange the event space — hotel, school, recreation centre, or customer boardroom.
- Obtain all necessary licences.
- Select any prizes to be awarded.
- Coordinate staff participation.
- Organize the clean-up.
- Distribute promotional information, such as mail-outs or registration forms.

4. HOLD THE EVENT
- Coordinate a reply system for confirmation of attendance — use a 1-800-number or fax line where possible.
- Use effective presentation, communication, and training skills to deliver the event.

5. CONDUCT THOROUGH FOLLOW-UP AFTER THE EVENT
- Create and send a follow-up letter thanking attendees.
- Solicit voluntary feedback with response cards or handouts at the event, or through a brief survey with the follow-up letter.

TRADE SHOWS

In many industries, trade shows are an important part of marketing and promotion. These events provide an opportunity to network with colleagues, suppliers, and competitors. In most cases, they offer a proven method for identifying suspect accounts — and, occasionally, for making sales. They also provide a desirable environment for launching or announcing new products and services.

Trade shows can help an organization improve its visibility in the marketplace and increase customer identification with its products and services. They are an important part of the business-creation process.

If you plan to participate in trade shows as part of your marketing and promotion activities, let's take a look at how you can make them successful.

◼ Planning

Planning for a trade show can be a time-consuming endeavour. There are many different types of shows to choose from — not all of which may be well suited to helping you reach your territory goals and objectives. So choose carefully. Identify the participants most likely to attend. Ask yourself if these people represent your target market.

As a rule, you should never go into a trade show just "hoping for the best." You should set objectives for the number of leads you expect, the number of sales you predict will result, and the bottom-line impact the show will have on territory profitability. By addressing these issues during the planning stages, you will have a benchmark against which you can compare the results afterward — and learn from what you see.

Be sure to incorporate your trade show activities into a wider strategy for communicating with customers and prospects. After all, if you don't let them know about it, they may not know the show exists or that you are exhibiting.

What about your booth or display? Consider the following guidelines.

- Select a theme for the booth — for example, *"Improving productivity in the '90s: The only way to survive!"*
- Specify a strategically beneficial booth location; here it helps to get your order in early because prime spots disappear fast. (In fact, many organizations order next year's space at the end of the current year's show.)
- Determine the layout of the booth, being sure to account for items such as equipment, electrical demands, brochures and table space, and samples.
- Design the backdrop and signs for the booth; use collapsible technology where possible.
- Organize transportation, shipping, electrical, compressed air, and insurance arrangements.

Once the planning has been completed, the next step usually involves getting organized for the show.

◄█ Logistics

There are two main areas to consider when organizing your booth for a trade show. Let's look at each of them in turn.

ORGANIZE MATERIALS AND RESOURCES

- Prepare materials, displays, and signs that will create attraction and excitement, drawing attendees into your booth.
- Select and acquire the best type of presentation technology.
- Prepare print, video, or computer materials, as required.
- Organize, schedule, and prepare other staff members.
- Train others how to manage the booth.

ORGANIZE/IMPLEMENT PRE-SHOW, SHOW, AND POST-SHOW ACTIVITIES

- Contact prospects and customers in advance; invite visitors to the booth.
- Make appointments with customers to be held at the booth.
- Invite local press and media.

- Take videos and pictures of booth and show, if appropriate.
- Organize a method for tracking attendance — a fishbowl for business cards, or a guest book, for example.
- Manage the flow of the booth. Based on expected traffic, specify the number of salespeople you want present. Use your consultative selling skills to establish relationships, uncover customer needs and objectives, qualify visitors as suspects (or not), and use your influencing skills to gain the customer's agreement to move forward in the sales process.

Following up

Most of the people who visit your booth may be deemed *suspects*. Those who don't visit remain in the the global market or your target market. Generally, these are the only classifications you need to consider — except in those rare situations where a visitor immediately qualifies as a *prospect*, or if you close a sale and secure a *customer*.

In order to reach the goals you set for the trade show, you should employ a thorough, immediate follow-up program. Every suspect visitor should hear from you within one month (preferably two weeks), either in writing, by telephone, or in person. Prompt follow-up is often required in order to move the suspect account "down the funnel" to become a genuine prospect. If not contacted promptly, a suspect may become uninterested — or worse, a new customer for your competition — thus falling out of the funnel.

If possible, before the show begins, prepare a post-show package to be sent to all suspect accounts. Then, once the show is over, you need add only a personalized letter to each package and it can be sent right away.

Try the Other Side of the Booth

You can often benefit significantly from attending trade shows — not as an exhibitor but as a visitor. Try attending those shows geared towards your target market (your customers' industries). The comparatively low price of a show pass is easily justified — and the return on investment could be enormous! Talk to your customers about their trade show activities, review local papers and announcements, and attend whenever possible — even if it's just for a short while. This will help you to foster goodwill with existing customers, thus reinforcing client relationships. It also can help you develop new business opportunities with suspect and prospect accounts.

MERCHANDISING PROGRAMS

In the consumer packaged goods, confection, food, and other industries, merchandising programs can be a large part of an organization's marketing and promotion efforts. In some cases, the responsibility for these activities falls squarely on the shoulders of the sales representative.

Essentially, merchandising programs concern the display of retail goods on the store shelf and the use of special displays, point-of-purchase materials, and in-store advertisements to enhance sales of your products.

Merchandising programs are typically based on improving consumer awareness and interest in your products. They have been studied and used for many years. There is a significant body of research data available on the science and psychology behind merchandising efforts. A full exploration of this science is clearly beyond the scope of this book; however, if merchandising is an important part of your business, then you should look for additional reading materials on this topic.

Even if your job doesn't involve merchandising, an understanding of the principles involved is still useful. So take some time to study the following principles.

- Coordinate point-of-purchase (POP) materials with your organization's national campaigns and advertising efforts (print and television).
- Design attractive drafts of product packaging graphics.
- Create appealing visual displays that draw the customer in closer.
- Plan store shelf assortments and layouts in desirable locations. Use focal points and concept areas. Generally speaking, a higher shelf location is better. Try to position your SKUs (stock keeping units) or shelf-space in order to maximize your competitive advantage.
- Track profitability per square foot of shelf space.
- Organize and maintain showrooms and displays where appropriate.
- Work closely with retailers, designers, and manufacturers in order to gather valuable consumer data and to refine merchandising efforts.
- Test-market products wherever possible. It can provide valuable information to both sales representatives and management.
- Organize and distribute any available promotional and product literature.

- Supplement supplier marketing programs with activities on a local level, such as personal appearances, talk shows, and contests.
- Establish consumer demand before launching new products through merchandising efforts — for example, talk about the product with customers and resellers.
- Organize and implement *"gift with purchase"* programs.

TELEMARKETING

One of the most popular methods for uncovering suspect accounts in a target market is through telemarketing programs. In fact, telemarketing is often the most effective type of marketing initiative. Why? Simply because it involves direct contact with the customer. This can improve the accuracy of identifying genuine suspect accounts.

Telemarketing programs offer a wide variety of other uses (apart from sales). Some examples include market research, customer service, customer surveys, price or product changes, and updates.

While the responsibility for conducting formal telemarketing programs usually falls to in-house specialists (or an outside agency), salespeople often become involved in program design or implementation. So it only makes sense that you understand some of the key components of an effective telemarketing program.

▬ Three steps to effective telemarketing

1. PLAN THE TELEMARKETING PROGRAM
As always, successful execution requires careful planning. Here are some of the steps you should consider in planning your telemarketing program.

- Visit other successful telemarketing sites for observation.
- Automate wherever possible.
- Investigate computer hardware and software.
- Identify your objectives; for example:
  - to conduct informal marketing;
  - to increase sales;
  - to generate suspect accounts;
  - to process orders; or
  - to provide customer service.

- Align program objectives with overall sales strategies and goals.
- Prepare a formal plan, including:
  - the target market on which you are focused;
  - the type of suspect client you want to attract;
  - the expected cost;
  - the expected response and conversion rates; and
  - the increase in profits you expect as a result of this program.
- Develop a critical path for implementation.
- Develop a script for callers, making sure that it uses effective communication skills and follows the consultative selling process.
- Stick to the goal of the call, whether it's to identify suspect accounts, conduct market research, or inform customers of a price increase; don't waste the customer's time.
- Prepare for success — have follow-up support mechanisms in place to fulfill telephone requests or process orders.
- Prepare and implement a pilot program; evaluate results.
- Adapt the final program accordingly.

2. IMPLEMENT THE TELEMARKETING PLANS
- Examine previously untried distribution avenues.
- Enter telephone lists and account information for identified suspect accounts into your customer database.
- Create history files for each suspect account to track calls and follow-up activities.
- Compile weekly and monthly reports (for extended programs) or a program summary (for contract projects).

3. DEVELOP AND IMPLEMENT COMPREHENSIVE FOLLOW-UP PLANS
As with trade shows, effective follow-up is important to the success of any telemarketing program. As a rule, you should contact identified suspects within two to four weeks (at the most). Here are some other issues to consider regarding follow-up efforts.
- Distribute the data you've obtained, such as customer requests or complaints.
- Respond to customers and advance the sales cycle.
- Measure results and evaluate the program.
- Generate new target opportunities and develop new objectives.

ADVERTISING

Some companies dedicate a great deal of their marketing and promotion budgets to advertising. This can take many forms, including print advertising, radio ads, television commercials, or sponsorships. In some industries, a company may also contribute funds to support their customers' advertising efforts. This is called "cooperative" or *co-op advertising*.

As a salesperson, you need to understand two principal rules of advertising. The first is that *all advertising must comply with company rules and applicable government legislation*. The second is that *advertising should generate a reasonable return on investment*.

Since you may be involved in the development of advertising or may be required to pre-approve customer ads, it's important that we review some of the general principles of advertising. These include regulatory issues, creative development, media selection, as well as measuring the effectiveness and costs of advertising in various media.

REGULATIONS

Any advertising with which you are associated must adhere to all prescribed regulations. This includes government legislation and industry guidelines, as well as company regulations. Be sure that you understand these areas thoroughly before undertaking any advertising project.

In Practice

Do you know your organization's advertising regulations? Investigate and write down your findings.

RETURN ON INVESTMENT

As noted earlier, any advertising effort should yield a reasonable return on investment. How do we ensure this? Ultimately, the return generated by any advertising campaign can be measured (and then with only a modest degree of accuracy) only after the advertising dollars have been spent. Even so, we can try to understand the actual mechanics of advertising in a variety of media. This will help us to identify the advertising that yields the greatest possible return on investment.

◼ Advertising 101

Some salespeople believe that no advertisement has ever sold a product or service. *"Salespeople sell products and services,"* they'll say. However, for most of us, the benefits of advertising are perfectly clear: with an effective advertisement, you can create product interest.

In order to achieve this goal, we need to define three things.

* to whom are we talking — the target market;
* what to say — the creative; and
* how to reach them — the media.

THE TARGET MARKET

We can assume that by now you have identified your organization's primary target markets. However, we should review this issue again for advertising purposes. Perhaps your advertising program needs only to focus on one component of your target market or maybe it should target an untouched market. In any case, to create an effective advertising campaign, you will need to define your target market very specifically.

THE CREATIVE

The message of your advertising campaign — the words themselves and their visual presentation — is obviously specific to the products or services being sold. In addition, the copywriting and design skills required are not something that can be taught here, although there are guidelines that copywriters and designers tend to follow. It is possible to learn more about designing effective advertising. If you feel it would be valuable for you to gain this knowledge, then invest in some library time, take a creative design course in advertising, or talk to some people in the field.

As a rule, you may rely on your experience, knowledge, and intuition when contributing to (or making) decisions about advertising design.

THE MEDIA

What media should you use to carry your message? Your choice will be determined by the following criteria.

- The number of people reached.
- The number of people reached who comprise the target audience.
- How often these people are reached.
- The cost of advertising in the medium.
- The cost of producing the message in the medium.
- The dominance that you (the advertiser) have in the medium.
- The effectiveness of the message.

Different types of media will meet these criteria to varying degrees. Generally, media can be classified according to the following measures:

Reach: the estimate of the percentage of the population in a defined area reached by an advertisement or commercial.

Frequency: the number of times that an advertising message is delivered.

Circulation: in print media, the number of copies of a publication delivered or purchased. In broadcasting, this refers to the coverage of a station.

In Practice

Using the illustration below as a guide, list five popular and five unpopular products available in the consumer marketplace today. Consider the advertising for each product. How much reach do you think it has? What percentage of the population do you think is familiar with the product?

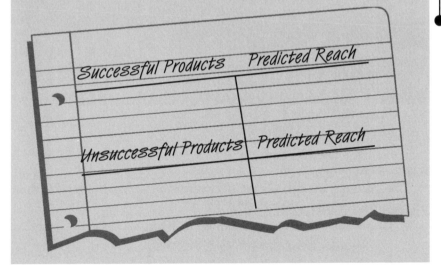

Successful Products	Predicted Reach
Unsuccessful Products	Predicted Reach

COST EFFICIENCY

A critical issue for any advertiser is the cost efficiency of a media buy. This is generally expressed in terms of how much you have to spend to deliver 1,000 messages, as shown by the formula below.

$$\text{Cost Per Thousand (CPM)} = \frac{\text{Total Cost}}{\text{Total Audience Reached}/1000}$$

MEDIA OBJECTIVES

What are the most important things to accomplish with your media selection?

1. The media must reach the target.

2. The media must deliver the message effectively.

3. The message should be conveyed with sufficient frequency to capture your audience's attention.

4. Considering the previous three, costs should be minimized in order to satisfy the second advertising principle: maximize return on investment.

Now ask yourself, *how can you accomplish this?*

1. Determine the *objectives* to be met through the media selection.

2. Decide on the *strategy* to be followed to meet those objectives, and formulate a *critical path* for implementation.

Some other questions that are wise to consider in determining the media to employ for an advertising campaign include:

- What media are compatible with the product and the distribution channel?
- Where is the competition advertising?
- What continuity is required?
- How flexible is the medium?

Be aware that media analysis can be complex. However, several firms are available to provide assistance. These organizations measure the various aspects of media effectiveness.

The Audit Bureau of Circulation (ABC) reports on circulation figures of daily newspapers.

The Bureau of Broadcast Measurements (BBM) reports facts on electronic media.

A. C. Nielson Company is similar to BBM.

Multi-Media Marketing

In today's rapidly evolving information age, more and more people are becoming comfortable with computers and new media. So it only makes sense that your marketing and promotion efforts embrace this technology — as well as advanced presentation technologies such as multimedia, video, and CD-ROM. Here are some of the new media that you might consider for your marketing and promotion activities.

USE THE INTERNET

- Experiment by opening an account with a service provider and explore the World Wide Web (WWW), e-mail lists, and news groups.
- Search the Internet for new suspects. But be careful! Internet users usually don't respond well to commercial solicitation. The Internet is not a business directory. Use proper "Netiquette" when on-line.
- Be aware of your customers on the Internet. Keep a list of them for reference.
- Use e-mail to keep customers informed of industry news.

USE THE LATEST TECHNOLOGIES

- Convert your marketing letters and documents to digital (computerized) format.
- Record market information on company computer systems for distribution internally and externally (codes, standards, policies).
- Use broadcast fax transmissions for direct mail campaigns (the delayed, mass-delivery of the same fax to a large number of different fax numbers).
- Use video or telephone conferencing where appropriate.
- Produce multi-media marketing materials, such as CD-ROM, floppy diskettes, and videos.
- Use multimedia effectively in sales, marketing, and promotional presentations.

KEEP CURRENT

- Participate in forums to gain new information.
- Read the business media for up-to-date ideas and information

FINALLY, BE SURE TO INVOLVE OTHER DEPARTMENTS IN MULTI-MEDIA MARKETING CAMPAIGNS.

Figure 17.1 (opposite page) outlines the key aspects of the four principal types of advertising media. Refer to this chart when making decisions about which one to select for a given project.

Some additional things to consider when developing an advertising campaign are shown in the box below.

Guidelines for Advertisers

1. Set advertising objectives. Clearly define the program goal — for example, promote a new product or service, or improve awareness of your organization. Determine what your expectations are, in quantifiable terms. Examples include: *an increased number of incoming calls*, or *increased sales*.

2. Set specific budgets before you start. Advertising can become quite costly very quickly. Set your financial limits ahead of time and stick to them. Determine your expected return on investment for each project.

3. Understand the various media channels and associated costs.

4. Establish the timing of your advertising efforts. Are there seasonal considerations? Should the advertising be linked with new product launches or other events at your company?

5. Look for advertising opportunities to help your customer improve sales, thus increasing the usage of your products and services. Turn these into co-op advertising opportunities, where you can provide support or financial assistance with the campaign.

6. Become intimate with your competition's advertising efforts.

7. Ensure that brochures, marketing letters, and other materials are customized to meet the unique needs of your clients and target market.

Finally, if you are involved advertising for your organization and territory, remember our original two principles:

- Comply with all government, industry, and company legislation, regulations, and guidelines for advertising.
- Maximize the return on investment gained from any advertising effort by considering: *whom to talk to*, *what to say*, and *how to reach them*.

Figure 17.1

Primary Advertising Media Characteristics

DAILY NEWSPAPERS	RADIO	TELEVISION	OUTDOOR ADVERTISING
PROS: • more dollars spent on newspaper advertising than any other media • distributed daily • high degree of advertising flexibility • choice of placement in publication allows for compatibility between product/service and media • penetrates all demographic groups • flat rate and open rate pricing available **CONS:** • beware of tight deadlines • must consider waste circulation when examining reach • low quality reproduction **CONSIDER:** • allow for enough white space in ad • headlines should not be in all capital letters • headline should entice readers into the ad • keep the message simple • don't hesitate to quote prices • be straightforward, don't be too clever • be specific, don't generalize	**PROS:** • 90% of Canadian adults listen to radio • uncomplicated; easy to buy/prepare material • flexible; changes can be made in mere hours • low costs allow for thorough coverage • very easy to target specific markets by selecting AM/FM, specific channels, time slots, when played (before news, after sports, during extended music play, etc.) • reach penetrates wide range of environments—in the car, in home, at work, etc. • stations have much information on the audience they reach at specific times of day **CONS:** • narrow reach • not visual • can be short, so information can be easily missed by listeners **CONSIDER:** • identify the target market you want to reach • analyze the relationship between time slots and reach demographics	**PROS:** • extremely effective appeals to multiple senses • 97% of Canadian households have a TV, and each one watches an average of over 5 hours per day • tremendous reach (potentially worldwide) • reaches all demographics • most researched advertising media **CONS:** • price—advertising space is extremely expensive to buy • price—TV advertising is extremely expensive to make • price—mistakes or refinements are extremely costly **CONSIDER:** • do you want to reach the largest possible audience or obtain frequency with a smaller audience—leads to air-time choices • demographics reached are determined by channels, time of day, during which show, etc.	**PROS:** • can reach wide range of demographics • visual representation • can achieve high frequency (commuters may see it every day, etc.) • various forms: posters, backlights, mall posters, superboards, spectaculars, junior posters, bus shelters, city benches, etc. **CONS:** • hard to target specific market • limitations on the message that can be conveyed • often ignored by audience **CONSIDER:** • brevity is important—should contain no more than five or six words • clarity is critical—use legible, serif type—people won't spend much time looking, so it must be clear • simplicity is crucial—try to express only one (maybe two) ideas • strive for immediate impact—use strong colour contrasts, appealing graphics and photos, etc. • be sure to include the name of the product and/or company in the ad

This chart highlights the pros, the cons, and the things to consider for each of the four, primary advertising media. Although sales professionals don't always get involved in the advertising decisions of their organizations, sometimes they do. And in some industries representatives provide advice to or manage co-op advertising for their customers. Therefore, it's valuable for sales professionals to have a basic understanding of the principles of advertising and media selection.

Summary

1, Today's salespeople are typically more than just order takers. They take active responsibility for managing a component of their employer's business — just as if they had a small business of their own. To be successful, they need to be relatively sophisticated business professionals, which requires (at least) an understanding of fundamental marketing principles. These salespeople take a proactive role in developing and implementing marketing activities within their own territory.

2. There are many small details to remember about each element of marketing and promotion. Refer to this chapter often when you become involved in these activities within your organization; it will serve as an excellent tool. This chapter serves to improve your awareness of the following types of marketing and promotion.

- regional and corporate marketing;
- networking;
- direct mail campaigns;
- education and training;
- trade shows;
- merchandising programs;
- market research;
- telemarketing programs; and
- advertising.

Review: Strategic selling skills

1. If you want to maximize performance and success, you should always strive to become not only an excellent *tactician* — that is, great at *influencing, building relationships with*, and *dealing with customers* — but also a supreme *strategist*. It's always worthwhile to undertake the planning and strategy development efforts outlined in this part of the book. If you don't, you may not realize your full potential.

2. In the real-life, working world, there often doesn't seem to be enough time for everything. Most of our time is spent dealing with customers, making sales presentations, negotiating purchasing agreements, and trouble-shooting problems. But it is still important to engage in strategic tasks such as completing sales reports, conducting territory S.W.O.T. analyses, forecasting the expected value of accounts, designing critical paths, and calculating the amount of time you can afford to spend with each prospective customer and still maximize profitability.

3. Given the increasingly competitive nature of the Canadian marketplace, strategic tasks are becoming more and more important in order to maximize territory returns. So, when you are faced with those situations where there just isn't enough time to do it all, deal with the urgent customer issues first, and remember to *think globally, act locally*.

4. Be sure that all of your activities and decisions are geared towards maximizing territory profitability. Every few minutes, stop and ask yourself: *"How is this leading to improved profitability?"* If you can't answer the question, shift your current efforts accordingly. Catch up on your strategic planning efforts — and don't wait too long.

5. In warfare, it is the tacticians who *conduct* the battles on the field and in the trenches. It is the strategists who *decide* where the tacticians should go and what they should do. To win the war, an army's tacticians and strategists must both be superior to those of the enemy. Either one alone is not enough. A superior tactician may overpower you; a superior strategist may outsmart you.

6. The warfare analogy holds true in today's business world. And the sales arena is like the battlefield where your opponent (the competition) is trying to win. So if you want to be successful, you must strive to be like the superior "army." When face to face with customers, you need to be better in the field than your opponents. And you need to be better in the planning room than the competition, developing goals and objectives along with the action plans needed to reach them.

Having completed this section of the book, you now have the tools and knowledge to become a superior strategist. The other parts have prepared you to become a winning tactician. So get out there and win the war!

References and Suggested Readings

Outlined below are the various reference sources used in developing this text. In addition, we have listed numerous complementary books and materials that may augment the topics examined herein. Each reference is recognized as a valuable resource, and you may benefit from any one (or all) of them. In reality, this list could have been voluminous. However, in the interest of time and space, we have restricted its contents to those materials considered immediately relevant.

Albert, Kenneth J. *How To Solve Business Problems*. New York, NY: McGraw-Hill Book Company, 1978.

Alessandra, Tony, Jim Cathcart, and John Monoky. *Be Your Own Sales Manager*. New York, NY: Prentice Hall Press, 1990.

Barnard, Sandie. *Rise Up, A New Guide To Public Speaking*. Scarborough, Ont.: Prentice Hall Canada, Inc., 1993.

Bender, Peter Urs. *Secrets Of Power Presentations*, Fifth Edition. Toronto, Ont.: The Achievement Group, 1991.

Blanchard, Kenneth H. *The Power of Ethical Management*. New York, NY: William Morrow and Company, Inc., 1988.

Blanchard, Kenneth H. *The One Minute Manager*. New York, NY: William Morrow and Company, Inc., 1982.

Cialdini, Robert B. *Influence, The Psychology of Persuasion*, Revised Edition. New York, NY: William Morrow and Company, Inc., 1993.

Covey, Stephen R. *Principle-Centered Leadership*. New York, NY: Simon & Schuster, 1990.

Covey, Stephen R. *The 7 Habits Of Highly Effective People*. New York, NY: Simon & Schuster, 1989.

Covey, Stephen R., A. Roger Merrill and Rebecca R. Merrill. *First Things First*. New York, NY: Simon & Schuster, 1994.

Dane, Les. *Surefire Sales Closing Techniques.* West Nyack, NY: Parker Publishing Company, Inc., 1971.

Dardik, Irving, and Denis Waitley. *Quantum Fitness: Breakthrough To Excellence.* New York, NY: Pocket Books, 1984.

Dessler, Gary, and Alvin Turner. *Human Resource Management In Canada,* Canadian Fifth Edition. Scarborough, Ont.: Prentice Hall, 1992.

Dolan, Robert J., ed. *Strategic Marketing Management.* Boston, Mass.: Harvard Business School Publications, 1991.

Farber, Barry J., and Joyce Wycoff. *Break-Through Selling.* Englewood Cliffs, NJ: Prentice Hall, Inc., 1992.

Fisher, James R., Jr. *Confident Selling.* West Nyack, NY: Parker Publishing Company, Inc., 1971.

Freed, Richard C., Shervin Freed, and Joe Romano. *Writing Winning Business Proposals.* New York, NY: McGraw-Hill, Inc., 1995.

Freeman, Lawrence H., and Terry R. Bacon. *Shipley Associates, Style Guide,* Revised Edition. Bountiful, Utah: Shiply Associates, 1990.

Hanan, Mack. *Consultative Selling.* New York, NY: AMACOM, a division of American Management Association, 1973.

Hanan, Mack, and Peter Karp. *Competing On Value.* New York, NY: AMACOM, a division of American Management Association, 1991.

Helmsetter, Shad. *You Can Excel In Times Of Change.* New York, NY: Pocket Books, 1991

Helmsetter, Shad. *The Self-Talk Solution.* New York, NY: Pocket Books, 1987.

Helmsetter, Shad. *What To Say When You Talk To Your Self.* New York, NY: Pocket Books, 1986.

Hersey, Paul, and Kenneth H. Blanchard. *Management of Organizational Behaviour: Utilizing Human Resources.* Englewood Cliffs, NJ: Prentice-Hall, Inc., 1982.

Hill, Napoleon, and E. Harold Keown. *Succeed And Grow Rich Through Persuasion.* Toronto, Ont.: Random House of Canada, Limited, 1970.

Koerper, Philip J. *How To Talk Your Way To Success In Selling*. West Nyack, NY: Parker Publishing Company, Inc., 1979.

Kolb, David A., Irwin M. Rubin, Joyce S. Osland, eds. *The Organizational Behavior Reader*, 5th Edition. Englewood Cliffs, NJ: Prentice Hall, 1991.

Lash, Linda M. *The Complete Guide to Customer Service*. Toronto, Ont.: John Wiley & Sons, Inc., 1989.

Maslow, Abraham H. *Motivation And Personality*, Second Edition. New York, NY: Harper & Row, Publishers, Inc., 1970.

McCready, Gerry B. *Professional Selling In Canada*. Toronto, Ont.: Holt, Rinehart and Winston of Canada, Limited, 1994.

Merrill, David, and Roger Reid. *Personal Styles And Effective Performance: Making Your Style Work For You*. Radnor, PA: Chilton, 1981.

Miller, Robert B., and Stephen E. Heiman, with Tad Tuleja. *Strategic Selling*. New York, NY: William Morrow and Company, Inc., 1985.

Miller, Robert B., and Stephen E. Heiman, with Tad Tuleja. *Conceptual Selling*. Walnut Creek, CA: Miller-Heiman, Inc., 1987.

Moine, Donald, and Kenneth Lloyd. *Unlimited Selling Power*. Englewood Cliffs, NJ: Prentice-Hall, Inc., 1990.

Moine, Donald, and John H. Herd. *Modern Persuasion Strategies*. Englewood Cliffs, NJ: Prentice-Hall, Inc., 1984.

Myers, Michele Tolela, and Gail E. Myers. *Managing By Communication*. New York, NY: McGraw-Hill, Inc., 1982.

Peters, Thomas J., and Robert H. Waterman, Jr. *In Search Of Excellence*. New York, NY: Harper & Row, Publishers, Inc., 1982.

Peters, Tom. *Thriving On Chaos*. Toronto, Ont.: Random House of Canada Limited, 1987.

Pickens, James W. *The Art of Closing Any Deal*. New York, NY: Warner Books Edition, 1989.

Porter, Michael E. *Competitive Strategy*. New York, NY: The Free Press, 1980.

Rackham, Neil. *Major Account Sales Strategy.* New York, NY: McGraw-Hill, Inc., 1989.

Rackham, Neil. *SPIN Selling.* New York, NY: McGraw-Hill, Inc., 1988.

Raiffa, Howard. *The Art And Science Of Negotiation.* Cambridge, Mass.: The Belknap Press of Harvard University Press, 1982.

Robbins, Anthony. *Unlimited Power.* Toronto, Ont.: Random House of Canada Limited, 1986.

Sabin, William A. *The Gregg Reference Manual,* Seventh Edition. Westerville, OH: the Glencoe Division of Macmillan/McGraw-Hill School Publishing Company, 1992.

Schiffman, Stephan. *Closing Techniques: Tips That Really Work!* Holbrook, MA: Bob Adams, Inc., 1994.

Seligman, Martin E. P. *Learned Optimism.* New York, NY: Alfred A. Knopf, 1991.

Stevens, Howard, and Jeff Cox. *The Quadrant Solution.* New York, NY: AMACOM, a division of American Management Association, 1991.

Tracy, Brian. *Advanced Selling Techniques: Master Newer, More Advanced Sales Tactics.* Niles, IL: Nightingale-Conant Corporation, 1994.

Tracy, Brian. *How to Sell Well.* Niles, IL: Nightingale-Conant Corporation, 1988.

Tracy, Brian. *Maximum Achievement.* New York, NY: Simon & Schuster, 1993.

Tracy, Brian. *Setting Business Strategy: Twenty-one Ideas for Success and Profitability.* Niles, IL: Nightingale-Conant Corporation, 1988.

Trailer, Barry. *Sales Mastery.* San Jose, CA: No Rush Publishing, 1991.

Truax, W. J. *Winning at Prospecting: The Art of Cold Calling Without Fear.* Chagrin Falls, OH: Trufield Enterprises, Inc., 1994.

Waitley, Denis. *New Dynamics of Winning.* New York, NY: William Morrow and Company, Inc., 1993.

Waitley, Denis. *The Psychology of Winning*. New York, NY: William Morrow and Company, Inc. 1990.

Walters, Dorothy M. *The Great Persuaders, Encyclopedia Of Sales*. Glendora, California: Royal Publishing Company, 1983.

Walther, George R. *Power Talking*. New York, NY: G. P. Putnam's Sons, 1991.

Williams, John C., and John A. Torella. *Success Retailing*. Toronto, Ont.: Retail Council of Canada, 1992.

Index